Turning My Pain t

(Sto

TURNING MY PAIN TO GAIN

STORY OF JOB

BIODUN OLAITAN

TURNING MY PAIN TO GAIN
The Story of Job

ISBN: 978-978-61590-2-7

Requests for information should be addressed to:
Nifepelumi@yahoo.co.uk
+447500048655

Printed by:
ScribeTribe Africa
BrownStone Estate,
Lekki, Lagos

www.scribetribe.media
hello@scribetribe.media
scribetribeafrica@gmail.com
+234(0)708-040-1080, +234(0)813-527-3602

Published in Lagos, Nigeria

This book is kindly dedicated to:

All those who are experiencing pain in their ministry, relationship, and/or body. There is comfort and peace at the end of your painful experience. Keep that dream alive don't give up.

Particularly to my spiritual parents, Pastor and Pastor Mrs E.A. Adeboye, who have survived several seasons of pains in life. Your lifestyle as mentors and leaders has taught me that pain is for a season, and the end of the matter is often better than its beginning, not because it's easier, but because its refined. I am inspired by one of your regular quotes: **"Death brings the final healing to every pain in life."**

I love you dearly Mummy and Daddy GO.

Foreword

Life inevitably brings seasons of suffering—moments when questions outweigh answers and pain clouds our perception of purpose. In such times, the Book of Job becomes more than ancient literature; it becomes a mirror, a map, and a mentor. *Turning Pain to Gain–Job* offers readers a timely and transformative journey through one of the Bible's most profound accounts of endurance, faith, and divine restoration.

This work masterfully unpacks the life of Job, not merely as a tale of trials but as a spiritual blueprint for turning adversity into advancement. It challenges believers to see suffering not as a sentence but as a setup for more profound revelation, refined character, and renewed purpose. Through biblical exposition, practical insight, and pastoral sensitivity, my brother and friend, Biodun Olaitan, invites us to examine our responses to pain—and more importantly, to recognise God's redemptive hand at work in every season.

As you read these pages, be prepared to confront uncomfortable questions, but also to receive supernatural comfort. Whether you are in the middle of your own "Job moment" or walking with others through theirs, this book will deepen your theology of suffering and strengthen your confidence in God's justice and mercy. Like Job, you may not get every answer, but you will encounter the One who is always faithful.

It is my prayer that this book will not only educate your mind but also enrich your spirit and encourage your soul, transforming pain into gain, sorrow into strength, and trials into testimonies.

Your brother in life's journey,

Seyi Oladimeji

Acknowledgements

This book has been long in the making. It has been a contribution of many known and unknown people who have been through a process of pain in life. It is impossible to mention you all, however I salute you all for forging through your season of pain.

My Eternal Source of grace, wisdom and light. My present Helper, Holy Spirit. To entire members of RCCG CRA COVENTRY, UK for privileged to lead and preach my heart to you by helping me to embrace my pains. My encouraging wife, children and grandchildren. My co-labourers in the ministry going through one form of pain in life, I salute you all for staying the course. May God continue to bless you all always.

I want to thank Josh Adeyemi, my writer. This book would not have been written without your help.

I am immensely grateful to Bright Ukwenga and the entire team at ScribeTribe Africa for their excellent publishing services.

Contents of this Book

Introduction

Pain is a universal experience, but its impact is deeply personal. It visits unannounced, disrupts without warning, and often leaves us grappling for meaning. Whether it arrives through loss, betrayal, sickness, or isolation, pain tests the fabric of our strength and the depth of our identity.

In its fiercest form, pain can become the crucible through which our most significant growth is forged. This is the heart of the *Turning Pain to Gain* series: a journey through the lives of biblical figures who faced unimaginable trials and emerged intact and transformed.

This third book centres on Job, a man whose story has echoed through generations as the embodiment of undeserved suffering. Job did not provoke disaster. He didn't trigger his loss. He lived with integrity, honoured others, and feared God. And still, calamity found him. It stripped him of wealth, children, health, and the comfort of understanding friends. But it could not strip him of his will to wrestle with grief. And in that wrestling, we find a mirror for our own.

Job's story doesn't offer easy answers. It doesn't always provide an immediate resolution. It offers a real-time chronicle of what it means to feel everything; anguish, confusion, abandonment, even anger; and still hold on. Not always perfectly. Not always with clarity. But with persistence.

This book is not written to elevate suffering, but to honour the journey of those who survive it. It's for the silent grievers, the stoic endures, the people whose prayers have gone unanswered, or at least in the ways they had hoped. It's for those who feel unseen in their pain, unheard in their questioning, and uncertain in their waiting.

In these pages, you won't find a glorified portrayal of triumph. You'll find a raw, human portrait of enduring hardship. You'll see how pain isolates, how grief bends our thoughts, how silence from others can be louder than words. You'll also see how hope survives in flickers. You'll see how a man reduced to ashes still speaks, questions, and reaches for something beyond explanation.

The goal of this book is not to turn Job into a hero for us to admire from afar. The goal is to walk beside him, to sit in the ashes with him, and to understand what it means to lose everything and still not lose yourself. Job's questions are our questions. His search for meaning mirrors ours. Ultimately, his restoration offers a whisper of what is possible when we refuse to let pain define us.

Throughout this book, we will journey through eight chapters that trace Job's movement from prosperity to devastation, through despair, and eventually toward restoration. Each chapter draws lessons not as moral imperatives but invitations to reflect, relate, and rise.

We begin with Job's prosperous life. It's essential to recognize that pain doesn't always follow wrongdoing. Sometimes it follows excellence. Job's life before the storm was marked by success and honour, making the subsequent fall even more jarring. It reminds us that pain doesn't discriminate. It doesn't check for guilt or innocence. It simply comes.

Then we move into isolation, the silence that followed his collapse. Friends who should have comforted him offered critique instead. And yet, this is familiar. Pain often exposes the limitations of our relationships. It reveals who can walk with us through the shadows and who only shows up when the sun shines.

From there, we explore Job's search for meaning. This is perhaps one of the most relatable aspects of his story. The deep yearning to understand why. Why now? Why me? Why this way? And though answers may not always come, the act of questioning itself becomes a part of healing. It is in the asking that we open space for understanding.

As Job wrestles internally, we see the pain's emotional and psychological weight. This isn't just a story of physical suffering. It's a story of mental anguish, of spiritual fatigue, of emotional breakdown. We watch a man walk through the spectrum of grief; from numbness to rage to resignation. And still, he does not give up.

Midway through, we see small flickers of hope, a word, a shift, and a moment of clarity. These glimpses don't erase the pain but light the path forward. They remind us that healing doesn't always begin with resolution. Sometimes, it starts with the decision to breathe again.

As Job prays for his friends, we witness the turning point. He doesn't condone their actions or pretend the hurt didn't happen. He chooses, instead, to rise above it, not out of weakness, but out of wisdom. This is where pain becomes purpose; when it teaches us how to be the person we needed.

Gratitude, then, becomes Job's weapon. He doesn't use it to deny reality, but to transform it. Gratitude doesn't erase loss, it reframes it. It gives us language for survival, for perspective, for growth.

Finally, we arrive at restoration, not just of possessions, peace, dignity, or vision. Job's end was greater than his beginning, not just in material wealth but emotional depth. He lived not just healed but whole.

If you are reading this and still in the ashes, know you are not alone. This book does not promise a quick fix. It promises a companion for the road and, hopefully, a reminder that pain, though sharp, can soften us into people of compassion, depth, and endurance.

Welcome to Job's journey. It is a journey of loss, yes, but more importantly, it is a journey of becoming.

Welcome to *Turning Pain to Gain.*

True character is not revealed in the height of success but in the depth of collapse.

chapter one
Prosperity Preceding the Storm

Job's life was a picture of stability; solid, unwavering, and admirable. Before the storm, he lived a life many would aspire to replicate. He was the kind of man who didn't just possess wealth; he possessed wisdom. He wasn't merely influential; he was deeply respected. His life was a rare fusion of abundance, integrity, material comfort, and spiritual conviction, but the true power of his story is not in the height of what he had; it is in the depth of what he would eventually lose.

There was a man in the land of Uz, whose name was Job; and that man was perfect and upright, and one that feared God, and eschewed evil. And there were born unto him seven sons and three daughters.

(Job 1:1-2)

Job's world was complete, and his household was bustling with life. He had ten children; seven sons and three daughters, who were alive and close-knit enough to dine together in celebration regularly. This was not just a family but a thriving, joyful community. Job's role as a father was not passive.

He actively interceded on behalf of his children, praying for their purity, making sacrifices, and showing an awareness of their outward behaviour and inward hearts. His spiritual depth was not performative; it was personal and persistent.

In terms of wealth, Job's portfolio was extensive. With thousands of livestock, numerous servants, and expansive property, he was the wealthiest man in the region. But his influence wasn't limited to possessions. He was known not for what he had, but for who he was. In his community, Job was a moral compass.

People sought his counsel. He was trusted, admired, and emulated. His success had depth; it wasn't hollow or hurried. It was earned, built on years of diligence, fairness, and character.

Job was also spiritually grounded. He was described as upright and blameless, not perfect, but consistently aligned with what was good, noble, and just. His reverence wasn't shallow. His relationship with the divine shaped his decisions, restrained his excesses, and humbled his heart. His prosperity had a moral backbone. It wasn't just about what he gained, but how he carried it.

This completeness, his family, wealth, influence, and spiritual maturity paint a portrait of a man who had every reason to feel secure. His life was a testament to what could happen when one lived rightly. And perhaps that is why what happens next feels so disorienting.

When someone who seemingly did everything right is hit with devastating loss, the world pauses. We expect storms to visit the reckless. We brace for collapse in the lives of the careless, but when tragedy strikes the faithful, we must confront a harder truth: that pain is not always a punishment.

Be sober, be vigilant;
because your adversary the devil,
as a roaring lion, walketh about,
seeking whom he may devour.

1 Peter 5:8

Job's pre-storm life matters, not to make us envy him but to help us understand the magnitude of his collapse. It sets the stakes and shows us what was on the line. His prosperity was not the highlight of his story, it was the platform from which his descent would shake the soul. By showing us, all that Job had, we prepare to feel deeply about all he would lose.

In this, we also prepare ourselves. Because, like Job, many of us have built good lives. We've worked hard, loved well,

and hoped sincerely. Yet, the storms still come. Sometimes without warning. Sometimes without explanation.
Job's story doesn't begin in pain. It begins in peace. That makes the pain so powerful and the restoration so profound.

This is where his journey, and ours, begins.

The Fragility of Good Seasons

A subtle danger comes with a life that seems to be going well. When things are steady, health is abundant, relationships are thriving, and resources are sufficient, we assume; often unconsciously, that the season will last.

Comfort lulls us into confidence. Security masquerades as permanence. Without realizing it, we begin to believe that our good days are evidence that we are somehow insulated from crisis.

This was the reality surrounding Job. His life gave no sign of impending tragedy. No warning lights were blinking, no dreams foretelling disaster, no moral compromise threatening collapse. From the outside, everything looked settled. From the inside, everything felt aligned, but prosperity, as beautiful as it is, can also be fragile. The danger lies in mistaking it for immunity.

We often equate stability with safety and abundance with approval. When we're doing well, we assume it means we're doing right. Sometimes we are, but the presence of blessing is not always a shield against pain. Some of the deepest trials come to those who seem most grounded, and when that happens, it's not just the loss that hurts—the shock.

People rarely expect pain at high points in their lives. It catches them off guard. It steals breath and reason. When the fall is from a great height, the impact is brutal. That's what makes the storm in Job's life so jarring. The contrast between what he had and lost couldn't be more pronounced. The higher the platform, the greater the fall.

For man also know not his time:
as the fishes that are taken in an evil net,
and as the birds that are caught in the snare;
so are the sons of men snared in an evil time,
when it falleth suddenly upon them.
Ecclesiastes 9:12

Many people wrongly believe that suffering is always tied to failure; that pain is proof that something was done wrong, but Job's story contradicts this. It shows us that pain can come even to the righteous.

Being upright doesn't prevent collapse. Doing everything right doesn't always yield the outcomes we expect. This truth can be unsettling but also freeing because it means that your pain isn't always punishment. It may simply be part of your human journey.

Pause momentarily and reflect on a settled season, your personal "before the storm." Maybe it was before the diagnosis. Before the phone call. Before the betrayal. Before the doors closed or the dream unravelled. Those moments were real, and the fall that followed didn't erase their beauty, but their sudden end may have left you with questions you still can't answer.

In that space between the prosperity we cherished and the pain we never saw coming, we begin to understand Job. His story is not distant. It is familiar. It is ours.

As we continue, we will walk the path from confidence to collapse; not to glorify suffering but to understand how profound loss shapes deeper faith and how brokenness can set the foundation for a new kind of strength.

The Suddenness of Collapse

It didn't happen gradually. There was no time to prepare. One minute, Job's world was intact; the next, it was unravelling. The messengers came in waves, each bearing news more devastating than the last. One by one, they arrived; out of breath, eyes wide with horror, voices trembling with urgency. The livestock was gone. The servants were slaughtered. His children were dead.

And then silence. The kind of silence that wraps around your throat and presses down on your chest. The kind that makes the world tilt beneath your feet. Job's world didn't just crack; it shattered.

The emotional weight of losing so much, so fast, is nearly indescribable. Grief didn't have time to settle before the next blow landed. There was no space for recovery, no moment to process, no breath between heartbreaks.

It was pain piled upon pain. And for anyone who's ever experienced a cascading collapse; losing a loved one while also losing a job, or facing betrayal while battling illness, Job's story touches a tender nerve.

What made it even more crushing was the speed. Everything he had known, everything he had built, fell apart in a blink. One moment he was managing abundance, the next he was managing ashes, and as the dust settled, Job was left standing amid the ruins of what used to be his life.

Be not afraid of sudden fear, neither of the desolation of the wicked, when it cometh. For the LORD shall be thy confidence and shall keep thy foot from being taken.
Proverbs 3:25-26

Perhaps you know what that feels like. Maybe your storm came without warning, a diagnosis, a message, a moment. Something shifted, and suddenly, the ground beneath you gave way. The people you leaned on disappeared. The plans you made disintegrated. And you were left staring at a future that no longer resembled what you imagined.

The pain of collapse isn't just in the loss; it's in the shock. The disorientation. The inability to catch your breath. Job didn't just lose possessions or people, he lost his rhythm. His sense of safety. He expected that good would continue.

Yet, there is something sacred in the ashes, not in what is lost but in what is left. In the moments when everything falls away, we discover what holds, what matters. Often, we discover parts of ourselves we never knew were there.

Job stood in that space. Broken, but not buried. Empty, but not erased. The storm had come, and everything had changed, but his story was far from over.

When Stability Turns to Shock

After the final messenger's words faded, the silence was deafening. In that moment, Job didn't scream. He didn't lash out. He didn't crumble to the ground in rage. Instead, he tore his robe, shaved his head, and fell to the ground, not in despair but reverence.

This reaction may seem strange. Unexpected, even. Because we expect people to shout when life unravels, we expect them to protest, curse, and collapse. And some do, but Job's first response was something deeper: it was the shock of a soul trying to breathe after being hit by a wave that stole its air.

Stability has a way of rooting us. It gives us patterns, rhythms, and confidence. We wake up daily and expect certain things to be in place, our routines, relationships, and realities. When those are snatched away suddenly, the soul enters a spiritual vertigo. Everything spins. Nothing feels real. In that place, grief doesn't rush, it hovers.

Then Job arose, and rent his mantle, and shaved his head, and fell upon the ground, and worshipped, And said, Naked came I out of my mother's womb, and naked shall I return thither: the LORD gave, and the LORD hath taken away; blessed be the name of the LORD.

Job 1:20-21

Job's reverence wasn't denial. It was the beginning of his

surrender. He was overwhelmed but not overcome. Shaken, but not shattered. The man who had just lost his children, his servants, and his livelihood didn't pretend it didn't hurt. He just chose to respond with reverence instead of rage.

That is where you may find yourself. You've been struck, perhaps not once, but repeatedly. The structures that made you feel safe have buckled. The people you trusted have disappeared. In the middle of the collapse, you find yourself quiet, not because you're strong, but because you're stunned.

This is where Job was, and this is where many of us often are. It's not weakness. It's the stillness that follows a quake. The moment when the dust hasn't even settled, and you're trying to piece together what just happened.

So, what do you do when the ground you stand on gives way? When all the things you leaned on are no longer there?

You breathe. You cry if you need to. You acknowledge the pain without letting it write the end of your story. You fall, not in defeat, but in surrender. Sometimes, the most sacred posture is where your knees hit the ground, not in weakness but in worship.

Job's story teaches us that even in the shock, even in the silence, there is space to honour what was lost while holding room for what might still be rebuilt.

The Pain of Losing Without Explanation

There's a particular kind of ache that comes with unanswered suffering. It's the space between what happened and why it happened, a gap that echoes with silence. Having lost everything he valued, Job wasn't offered a reason. No divine whisper. No cosmic explanation. Just silence.

This lack of clarity didn't just compound his pain; it redefined it. Without a reason, the suffering wasn't just physical, emotional, or financial, it became existential. It questioned the structure of justice, the reliability of faith, and the point of righteousness.

Job's pain wasn't merely about what he lost but also about the absence of meaning behind the loss. Humans crave explanation. We want to connect dots, to understand patterns, to assign reasons. When tragedy hits, the first question is often, "Why?" And when no answer comes, the silence can be more deafening than the loss itself.

For Job, there was no clear enemy to blame. No evident mistake to correct. His world unravelled without provocation, and that's what makes his story so universally human. Because sometimes pain comes uninvited, unexplained, and seemingly undeserved. And when it does, it forces us to confront our understanding and control limits.

For those walking through a season like this, Job offers a strange kind of comfort. Not because he triumphed quickly, but because he stayed. He stayed in the questions. He remained in the conversation. He didn't shut down or numb out. He processed. He mourned. He questioned. And somehow, through that process, he endured.

The LORD is nigh unto them that are of a broken heart; and saveth such as be of a contrite spirit.
Psalm 34:18

It's okay not to have the answers. It's OK to feel the weight of confusion. What matters is that you keep walking. You should allow the questions to shape you, not harden you. That you make space for pain to be real, and for growth to be possible; even in the dark.

Job's loss may have begun with tragedy, but his journey becomes a profound exploration of what it means to be human in a world where not everything makes sense, and that, too, is sacred ground.

Soul Searching

As you read this, you may find echoes of Job's story in your own. Perhaps it was a phone call that changed everything. A diagnosis that shattered plans. A betrayal you never saw coming. Or maybe it was a slow unravelling, one missed opportunity, one silent grief at a time. Sudden or slow, loss rewrites our story.

Take a moment to name your storm. What was your "everything is gone" moment? Was it the death of a loved one? The implosion of a relationship? The crumbling of a career you poured your life into? Or maybe the quiet erosion of your self-worth as life chipped away at your confidence?

This is not to relieve your pain, but to invite you to sit honestly with it.

Ask yourself:

- What did I cling to for safety that no longer exists?
- What did I lose that felt irreplaceable?
- What do I fear I'll never recover from?

These are not just questions, they are gateways. Because asking them with honesty begins the journey of recovery. And like Job, you don't need to have the answers yet. You just need the courage to start.

Help, LORD; for the godly man
ceaseth; for the faithful fail from
among the children of men.
Psalm 12:1

Foreshadowing the Journey Ahead

Job's story does not end in the ashes. It begins there. What feels like devastation is the prologue to something deeper, wiser, and ultimately more beautiful.

There will be wrestling, silence, unanswered questions, and delayed comfort, but there will also be growth, transformation, and restoration; not necessarily back to what was but forward into something stronger.

Job will not walk alone, and neither will you.

So as we turn the page, we invite you not to rush through the pain, but to walk with it, to meet yourself in it. Because in the end, the goal is not just survival. It's becoming.

When suffering is at its loudest, the silence of friends can echo the most

chapter two
The Silence of Support

The Collapse of Comfort

After the wave of loss, Job found himself in a place few can fully imagine but many have brushed against the hollow, silent, aching aftermath of catastrophe. Everything that once defined his world, his children, his wealth, his physical well-being-had been taken in the most brutal sequence of events.

There was no time to grieve one loss before another arrived. And now, in the wake of that storm, there was only pain. No explanation. No relief. Just ashes, silence, and sorrow.

Emotionally, he was wrecked. His grief wasn't abstract, it was visceral. The kind that steals sleep and turns even breathing into labour. Grief clouded his vision and strangled his hope. Physically, he was deteriorating.

Sores covered his body. His health had betrayed him. Spiritually, he was shaken by what had happened and the absence of divine explanation. He had always lived in moral clarity, guided by faith and principles. And now, all of that seemed to mock him.

And the LORD said unto Satan, Behold, he is in thine hand; but save his life. So went Satan forth from the presence of the LORD, and smote Job with sore boils from the sole of his foot unto his crown.

Job 2:6-7

In this fragile state, Job's friends arrived. On the surface, their coming should have brought comfort. After all, these people knew him for his strength. Who had once dined with him in his abundance. Who had sought his wisdom, admired his fairness, and leaned on his stability. It should have been them if anyone could hold him in his weakness.

For a moment, their presence did provide some sense of solace. They sat with him. They saw the extent of his suffering and chose silence, perhaps out of reverence or helplessness. They tore their clothes and sprinkled dust on their heads, a symbol of shared grief. It was a gesture that said, "We see your pain. We are here."
That moment didn't last.

What began as solidarity slowly mutated into suspicion. The longer they sat, the more they seemed to search for answers, not to comfort Job, but to rationalize his suffering.

Their need to make sense of the pain outweighed their commitment to sit with it simply. And so, what should have been comfort became confrontation. Support gave way to scrutiny.

Rejoice not against me, O mine enemy:
when I fall, I shall arise; when I sit in darkness,
the LORD shall be a light unto me.
Micah 7:8

This shift mirrors the experience of many people today. Friends and loved ones often show up after a tragedy. At first, they offer the right words, gestures, and presence. But over time, their discomfort with your ongoing pain reveals itself.

Their patience thins. Their empathy wears out. And in its place comes advice, judgment, and questions disguised as concern: "What did you do to deserve this?" "Maybe you're not praying enough." "Are you sure you didn't bring this on yourself?"

We want our friends to be safe spaces; to stand by us, not just visit our suffering. But often, the people we expect to support us reveal their limitations. Their inability to handle our grief exposed something we hadn't seen before: their friendship was conditioned on our strength. Our suffering unsettles them. And in trying to manage their discomfort, they distance themselves, or worse, blame us.

This is the collapse of comfort: when the people who should be your refuge begin to sound like your accusers.

Present But Not Supportive

Job's friends stayed silent for seven days. That number is striking. In ancient culture, seven days of mourning were customary, reserved for only the most devastating losses. Their silence wasn't passive, it was ritual, an attempt at shared mourning.

In that silence, there was perhaps an early glimmer of understanding. Sometimes, there are no words. Sometimes, just being there matters.
But silence is a strange thing. It can mean many things. Sometimes, it speaks of reverence, restraint, avoidance, or judgment. And when the silence breaks, we understand what kind of it was.

A friend loveth at all times,
and a brother is born for adversity.
Proverbs 17:17

When Job's friends finally spoke, the floodgates of assumption opened. Their speeches were long, impassioned, and theologically sound by the standards of their time. But they were not helpful. Their central message was clear: Job, you must have done something to deserve this.

Imagine the psychological weight of that. You are at your lowest point. You are physically wrecked, emotionally exhausted, and spiritually disoriented. And the people closest to you begin to explain your suffering not as misfortune, but as a consequence. Their presence, once comforting, becomes crushing.

This is not unfamiliar to many. You may recall times when people surrounded you but still felt profoundly alone, when no one said the wrong thing, but no one said the right thing either, when the air was filled with silence, yet the silence screamed of judgment, or worse, when the silence ended and the words that followed felt like betrayal.

Support is not just presence. It is presence with intention, presence with empathy, presence that says, "I don't understand this, but I won't abandon you in it."

Some people sit beside you in pain and hold your hand. Others sit and try to dissect it. Job got the latter.

Rejoice with them that do rejoice,
and weep with them that weep.
Romans 12:15

There is a difference between being there for someone and being with someone. One observes, the other engages, one offers analysis, and the other offers heart. Job's friends were present, but they were not supportive. Their need to be right, explain, and theologize overpowered their ability to be simple.

Empathy is silent when words would wound. It listens when explanations aren't needed. It holds space rather than filling it. Judgment, on the other hand, often dresses itself as counsel. It claims to be helpful, but it distances the pain from the person. It makes the sufferer feel responsible for their suffering. That's what Job faced.

He was not just surrounded by silence. He was surrounded by people whose silence gave way to assumptions, people who couldn't reconcile his pain with their belief system and so concluded he must be the problem.

Being surrounded but alone is one of the cruellest forms of isolation. You hear voices, but none speak for you. You see faces, but none reflect your anguish. You're not invisible, but you are unseen.

It is better to trust in the LORD
than to put confidence in man.
Psalm 118:8

Job didn't crumble. He began to speak, not just to his friends but also to his grief and confusion and, eventually, to his God. In that choice, he models something powerful: when support fails, the voice within must rise.

When Words Wound More Than Help

There are moments in life when silence is not only sacred but necessary. When someone is reeling from tragedy, the words that follow matter sincerely. They can be salve or salt, healing or harming. Unfortunately for Job, the words from his friends were not healing.

Initially, their silence may have communicated empathy. But when they broke it, they broke something else too, the fragile trust between sufferer and supposed supporter. The words came, and with them came judgment, moral analysis, and theological conclusions that pierced deeper than the loss itself.

There is that speaketh like the piercings
of a sword: but the tongue of the wise is health.
Proverbs 12:18

His friends, Eliphaz, Bildad, and Zophar, took turns speaking into Job's pain with explanations he never asked for. Instead of acknowledging his suffering and standing with him in solidarity, they assumed a cause-and-effect framework: "You must have done something wrong. God must be punishing you. No one suffers like this without a reason."

They were trying to help, but not every attempt to help is

helpful.

In times of deep grief, well-meaning people often reach for explanations. They try to find a purpose, a hidden logic, a divine lesson; anything to make sense of what feels senseless. And in doing so, they may offer statements that, rather than comfort, compound the pain:

- "Everything happens for a reason."
- "Maybe this is a test."
- "God gives his hardest battles to his strongest soldiers."
- "You must have opened a door."

While these words may sound spiritual or wise, they often feel like accusations in the moment of suffering. They assign responsibility where none may exist. They imply that the sufferer had control over what happened. And that can be devastating.

The tongue holds incredible power. With it, we can affirm or alienate, lift or crush. Words are not neutral. They echo in the soul long after they are spoken. A kind word spoken at the right time can become an anchor for someone drowning. A careless or judgmental word can become a weight that drags them deeper.
Here are some of the damaging words that Job's friends delivered can cause:

1. **Shame**: Words that imply fault where there is none can cause a person to internalize guilt and shame they were

never meant to carry.

2. **Isolation**: Judgmental words can push the sufferer further into isolation, making them feel misunderstood and alone.
3. **Self-doubt:** When those you trust suggest your pain is your fault, you begin to question your worth, decisions, and even your sanity.
4. **Bitterness**: Repeated judgment can harden the heart, breeding resentment toward people, life, and God.
5. **Delayed Healing**: Instead of helping someone process grief, hurtful words can create emotional wounds that take longer to heal than the original loss.
6. **Anger and Rage:** Feeling judged in your most vulnerable state can lead to suppressed anger that later erupts or quietly corrodes your soul.
7. **Spiritual Confusion:** When suffering is linked to divine punishment or others' sins, it can lead to spiritual disillusionment and confusion.

Job didn't just suffer loss, he suffered blame, and that blame came from the very people who should have offered grace.

Many people may find this painfully familiar. You expected comfort but received critique. You looked for someone to hold your hand, and they handed you judgment instead. The people who should have been a cushion became another weight.

What Job needed was someone to listen. To sit with him in the ash heap. To cry with him. To affirm, "I don't understand this either, but I'm not going anywhere."

What he got instead was speculation wrapped in spiritual arrogance.

Compassion doesn't demand answers. It offers presence. It says, "You don't have to go through this alone," and often, it's the absence of that kind of compassion that makes pain feel unbearable.

If you've experienced words that wounded more than they helped, know this: it wasn't your fault. And you don't have to carry those words into your future. They were not true. They were fear, insecurity, and discomfort disguised as advice.

If you are supporting someone in pain, choose your words wisely. Or choose silence. Because in moments of great suffering, what people need most is not your wisdom. It's your witness.

The Human Need for Safe Spaces

We instinctively reach for something or someone to hold onto when life falls apart. It's human nature. We were not designed to face devastation alone. Our minds long for clarity, our hearts long for company, and our spirits crave shelter. In those moments when everything we relied on collapses, we look for what remains. Often, we hope it will be the people we trust.

For Job, the ash heap wasn't just physical but relational. The same community that once celebrated his wisdom now questioned his integrity. His closest companions didn't understand his pain, and rather than admit their confusion, they tried to explain it away.

It is a lonely thing to suffer in public. It is lonelier still to be misunderstood in your suffering.

We all need safe spaces. Not perfect ones—just safe ones. A place or person where we don't have to explain our pain. Where tears aren't questioned. Where silence is honoured. Where presence outweighs solutions.

When my father and my mother
forsake me, then the LORD will take me up.
Psalm 27:10

What happens when even those spaces betray us? When the people we expected to sit with us instead step away, or worse, speak against us?

For many, that disappointment is more crushing than the initial loss. It's one thing to hurt. It's another to hurt while being blamed. When friends minimize your grief or turn it into a lecture, they don't just miss the mark; they deepen the wound.

So what do you do when even your friends don't understand?

1. **Grieve the loss of that expectation:** It's okay to mourn not just what happened to you, but who wasn't there when it did. Disappointment deserves its moment of grief. Let yourself feel it, name it, and release it.

2. **Seek emotional safety elsewhere:** Support can come from unexpected places; a counsellor, a new friend, a spiritual mentor, a support group. If one well runs dry, don't stop seeking water. Safe spaces exist. Sometimes you just must look in unfamiliar places.

3. **Lower the expectation, not your worth:** People failing you doesn't mean you're unworthy of care. It just means they couldn't offer it. Don't let their shortcomings redefine your value.

4. **Strengthen your internal support system:** This might be a season where you have to become your anchor. You create inner stability when the outside world goes silent through journaling, prayer, meditation, reflection, or simply affirming your voice.

5. **Draw boundaries with those who hurt you:** You can still love people from a distance. Compassion doesn't

require closeness. Protect your peace. Just because someone meant well doesn't mean they're healthy for you.

The danger of expectation is that it often sets us up for disappointment. We assume people will respond the way we would, that they will stay when it gets uncomfortable, and that they will understand without needing an explanation, but expectations are fantasies we haven't communicated. When they go unmet, the resulting disappointment can feel like betrayal.

Job expected his friends to listen, to care, to stay open. Instead, they accused him. Their words weren't just hurtful; they betrayed the friendship they once shared.

That's what isolation does in pain; it magnifies everything. Every silence feels louder. Every word feels heavier. Every absence feels sharper.

Still, there's a lesson buried in this part of the story. Sometimes, the absence of others reveals the presence of something deeper in us. When safe spaces aren't given, we learn how to build them. When comfort isn't offered, we know how to comfort ourselves.

Job was stripped of everything, including relational support, but in that vacuum, something grew: a voice, resilience, and clarity.

Emotional and Spiritual Isolation

There are seasons in life where loneliness wears more than one face. It's not just about being physically alone; it's about feeling unseen, unheard, and untouched by comfort. Job's suffering reveals this complex isolation, one that runs on multiple tracks at once: emotional, relational, and spiritual.

Emotionally, Job was in freefall. Grief had gripped every part of his being. The loss of his children wasn't just about their absence; it was about the severing of a deep emotional tether. These were not mere figures in his life; they were his joy, legacy, laughter, and light.

Losing them in one day was to knock the emotional air out of Job. Add to that the physical torment of his failing health, and Job's emotions were unravelling. The man who once offered wisdom now sat silently, scraping his wounds with broken pottery. That image alone is a portrait of despair.

And he took him a potsherd to scrape himself withal; and he sat down among the ashes. Then said his wife unto him, Dost thou still retain thine integrity? curse God, and die.
Job 2:8-10

Relationally, he was abandoned or misunderstood by everyone who mattered. The same friends who once honoured his insight now questioned his morality. His wife, overwhelmed by the horror of it all, asked him why he still held on to his integrity.

The community that once revered him stood back, unsure what to say, or worse, whispering their conclusions from afar. It's a specific kind of heartbreak to realize that the people you loved most, the ones who celebrated you in your high seasons, are unable or unwilling to walk you through your low ones.

Then there was the spiritual silence.

Job's connection to the divine, which had always been a steady foundation, now felt distant. It's not that he lost faith; it's that he couldn't feel faith. There were no signs. No dreams. No divine words of reassurance. Just a heavy, suffocating quiet. That's one of the most challenging aspects of suffering; the silence of God in the middle of it.

Many who have endured deep pain know this well. They know what it means to pray and hear nothing in return. To ask, "Why?" and be met with stillness. Go from feeling God as a near presence to wondering if He's paying attention. That shift can feel like abandonment. And while theology may say otherwise, pain doesn't always care about theology. It just knows how it feels.

Job was alone on all fronts. Emotionally bruised. Relationally disappointed. Spiritually distanced. And that is where layered loneliness becomes unbearable, because it's not just one loss, it's a collapse of every kind of support you thought you had.

This layered loneliness is not uncommon. People lose someone they love, and friends start pulling away because they don't know what to say. Others face medical or financial crises and discover how quickly people disappear when help is needed. And for many, God feels far away in the middle of that isolation, like a light just out of reach in a pitch-black tunnel.

The weight of this loneliness isn't always loud. Sometimes it's quiet and heavy. It settles into your chest like a permanent ache. It shows up at night when there's no one left to talk to. It wakes you in the morning and greets you before your feet touch the floor.

Turn thee unto me and have mercy upon me; for I am desolate and afflicted. The troubles of my heart are enlarged: O bring thou me out of my distresses. Look upon mine affliction and my pain; and forgive all my sins.
Psalm 25:16-17

It's not just the absence of people, it's the absence of connection. And even when others are physically present, the feeling remains: No one sees me. No one understands.

Job's story gives voice to that kind of isolation. It doesn't rush to fix it. It doesn't paint over it with quick hope. It just names it. And in doing so, it permits you to name it too.

You're not alone in feeling alone. You're not weak for wondering where everyone went. You're not faithless for asking where God is. You're human, and your longing for connection in suffering is not a flaw, it reflects the divine image within you, wired for community.

There's power in naming loneliness, not staying in it but beginning to walk through it.

What Job Needed But Didn't Get

In his most vulnerable moment, Job needed very little, yet he needed everything. He didn't require explanations. He didn't need theology. He wasn't searching for answers. He needed what every human being in deep pain longs for: listening, presence, and compassion.

Listening: Listening is not about preparing a reply, it's about giving someone space to be fully seen and heard. When a person is in pain, being listened to is healing. It validates the experience. It says, "You matter. Your pain is real." Job's friends, however, didn't listen. They heard his groans, and instead of sitting quietly with him in his lament, they began building arguments. Their ears were open, but their hearts were not.

Presence: True presence doesn't always come with words.

Sometimes, the most powerful thing a person can do is simply be there, sit beside someone in silence, hold their hand, offer a steady gaze. That kind of presence anchors the sufferer in a chaotic world. Initially, Job's friends showed up and sat with him in silence. But their presence became poisoned when they spoke, revealing that their motives were rooted not in comfort but in correction.

Compassion: Compassion is not about solving the pain, it's about sharing it. It's the willingness to feel a fragment of what the other is feeling. Job didn't need people to fix him. He needed people to grieve with him. Instead, he was interrogated, judged, and treated as if his losses were logical consequences of secret sin.

Job needed what many of us need in hard times: someone to sit without fixing, cry without analysing, and stay without withdrawing.

He didn't get it.

That gap, the space between what we need and receive—can be one of the most painful parts of suffering. It adds insult to injury. It shifts the pain from the event to the people. And for many, that's a familiar feeling. Maybe you've been through something devastating, and the people you thought would hold you up walked away. Or worse, they blamed you. They spiritualized your sorrow. They turned your pain into a lesson.
Modern-day versions of Job's experience sound like:

- "Maybe God is teaching you something."
- "You must have done something to open the door."
- "Are you sure you didn't bring this on yourself?"

When advice replaces empathy, the wounded become more isolated.
Job needed empathy, so he received a theology, a shoulder, and a sermon. And for many, this pattern continues.

But the beauty of Job's story is that even when others failed him, he didn't forget himself.

Finding Strength in Isolation

Despite being misunderstood, misjudged, and mishandled by his friends, Job didn't collapse into self-pity. He didn't adopt their view of his suffering. He didn't allow their misinterpretation of his story to become his truth.

He stood.
Not with bravado. Not with bluster, but with a quiet kind of courage, the kind that sits in ashes and still dares to speak.

There are times in life when we must stand alone. Not because we want to, but because no one else can stand with us. In those moments, we are invited to discover something deeper: our inner voice.
The inner voice isn't always loud. It doesn't shout over

the noise of judgment. It doesn't compete with external criticism. It waits. It whispers. And it reminds you who you are.

Here's how to begin hearing it:

1. **Create space for stillness.**
   Your inner voice is hard to hear in chaos. Quiet your environment long enough to listen to what your soul says through journaling, meditation, solitude, or reflection.
2. **Challenge the external narrative.**
   Just because others say something doesn't mean it's true. Ask yourself: "Is this my truth or someone else's assumption?" Separate opinion from reality.
3. **Speak affirmations rooted in identity.**
   Remind yourself: "I am not my circumstance." "I am not what happened to me." "I am not the failure others see." Even if you don't fully believe it, saying it starts the healing process.
4. **Embrace your story without shame.**
   Isolation offers clarity, reveals who's there for you, and shows your resilience. Accept your scars. They are signs of survival, not symbols of shame.

When human support fails, it's not the end. It can be the beginning of deeper self-knowledge and unexpected strength. Job's friends failed him, but in their failure, Job found his voice. He challenged their assumptions. He maintained his integrity. He spoke to God, even when God was silent.

That's the invitation to you, too.

If no one else claps for your endurance, clap for yourself. If no one else sees your pain, see it and honour it. If no one else supports you, become your safe place. Isolation is real, but so is the strength that grows in it.

Reflection and Transition

Job's story, up to this point, isn't wrapped in answers. It's soaked in questions, aches, and quiet confrontations with disappointment. The people who should have helped didn't. The faith that once felt firm now trembles. And the silence from God and others feels louder than any comfort could.

In the middle of all that silence, something resilient begins to rise: a voice, a question, a reaching. The job does not collapse inward. He leans into the pain. He begins to search, not just for relief but for meaning.

Now, pause here, before we move ahead, reflect on your own experience:

- Have you ever expected support and instead met silence or blame?
- Have you felt the ache of being surrounded by people

but still utterly alone?

- Have you grieved not only what was lost, but also who didn't show up?

These aren't just rhetorical questions, they are invitations. To name your disappointment. To acknowledge the wounds that didn't come from events but from people, begin untangling yourself from the weight of those unmet expectations.

Because here's the truth: your healing does not depend on everyone understanding you. Your progress does not hinge on their permission. You are allowed to keep going even when your support system caves in.
Job's voice, though battered, is still his own. His pain, though deep, does not swallow him. And that same grit lives in you.

As we turn the page, Job will begin a deeper journey, not just of grief but of questioning, wrestling, and seeking something beyond human understanding.

The silence may not break immediately, and the support may never return, but the voice within the one who knows you were made for more will grow louder.

“

Meaning isn't always found at the end of the road, sometimes, it's uncovered with every uncertain step

chapter three
Searching for Meaning
The Echo of "Why?"

Job sat in the dust, surrounded by loss, abandoned by comfort, and covered in silence. His body ached, his heart broke, and his mind spiralled with a question older than language: Why?

Why did this happen? Why so suddenly? Why me? Why now? Why like this?

The echo of "why" is one of the most human responses to pain. It's not a sign of rebellion or spiritual failure, it's evidence of the mind trying to reconcile chaos with order, suffering with meaning. Once revered for his insight, Job found himself without any answers. But he refused to silence the questions.

That refusal is essential.

In many faith traditions, questioning is often seen as weakness, doubt, or disobedience. But that's not what Job models for us. Job's questions were not an exit from faith, they were the very expression of it. He brought his agony into the open. He didn't curse under his breath or pretend he was fine. He cried out; not in polished language but in raw, honest desperation.

This chapter of Job's journey reminds us that asking questions doesn't mean abandoning belief. It means living authentically. Pain demands honesty. And honesty includes not knowing.

To question is to reach. It's to admit you care enough to wrestle. Job wasn't trying to escape his pain; he was trying to make sense of it. And so he asked.

If you're reading this and asking your own "why?" you are not alone. Maybe your questions sound like:

- Why did they leave?
- Why did this diagnosis come?
- Why did I lose what I worked so hard for?
- Why does it feel like everyone else is moving forward while I'm stuck?
- Why did God let this happen?

These questions are sacred, not because they always have answers, but because they honour your humanity. They name your pain. And they create space for connection with yourself, others, and the divine.

Job's cries into the silence didn't remove his suffering, but they preserved his sanity. He held onto his right to question in a world where everything was taken. You have that right, too.

Not every prayer must be praise, and not every conversation with God must be confident. Sometimes, faith sounds like a whisper: "Why?" In that whisper, something true begins to rise.

Wrestling with the Unseen

As Job's questions multiplied, so did his sense of disconnection, not just from people, but from God. What once felt close now felt distant. What once brought comfort now brought confusion. And yet, Job kept talking. He kept directing his words into the void, the heavens, and the unseen.

This is what it means to wrestle with the unseen.

It is the act of holding on when nothing is holding you back. Of praying into silence. Of trusting when trust feels foolish. Of pouring out your thoughts with no immediate assurance that anyone is listening. And still, you speak.

Job's faith wasn't clean or polished. It was raw and restless. He didn't pretend. He didn't sugarcoat. His belief was battered but, not broken. That kind of faith survives the storm, not because it understands, but because it refuses to let go.

Doubt and faith are not opposites. Often, they walk side by side. To question is not to betray your beliefs; it's to dig deeper into them. Job never denied God's existence. He just didn't understand God's silence. That's a very different posture than rejection. It's a cry for a relationship; a longing to be heard.

How long wilt thou forget me, O LORD? for ever?
how long wilt thou hide thy face from me? How long shall
I take counsel in my soul, having sorrow in my heart daily?
how long shall mine enemy be exalted over me?
Psalm 13:1-2

Many people know this feeling: wrestling not with what happened but with the absence of response. They pray and hear nothing. They wait and see no movement. They cry out and feel invisible, but wrestling is sacred. It means you haven't given up. It means you care enough to struggle. It means the relationship still matters.

Wrestling with the unseen teaches us a quieter kind of strength. It is not the strength to move mountains, but the strength to keep walking when the mountain doesn't move. It is the strength that believes even when it doesn't feel.

Job didn't stop talking. He didn't stop hoping. He didn't

stop reaching, and through that persistence, something shifts, not in the circumstances, but in the man himself.

When Answers Don't Come

One of the most complex parts of suffering is the silence that follows our questions. Job cried out, not once but repeatedly. He looked for answers in his pain, his memories, his theology, and his prayers. And yet, heaven seemed quiet.

This kind of divine silence creates a unique frustration. It's not just about not knowing. It's about being left in suspense, with your heart wide open and your pain unanswered.

Here are some of the frustrations that come with silence:

- The frustration of invisibility: You wonder if your pain even matters. If God sees it. If anyone does.
- The frustration of abandonment: When prayers go unanswered, it can feel like you've been forgotten or left behind.
- The frustration of overthinking: Without answers, your mind fills in the blanks—usually with fear, guilt, or false conclusions.
- The frustration of delay: Time stretches. You wait for a sign, a word, a shift. And when it doesn't come, you feel like healing will never arrive.

- The frustration of watching others move on: While you're stuck in grief or confusion, others seem to flourish, which only sharpens the sting of your waiting.

Job felt all of this. He wasn't just grieving his losses; he was grieving the silence. He wanted dialogue, but instead got distance, but meaning isn't always immediate. Some answers don't arrive on schedule; sometimes, the lessons take shape long after the pain has passed.

So, what can we do when answers don't come?

1. **Hold space for the unknown:** You don't have to resolve everything right now. You can carry questions and still move forward. Permit yourself not to know.
2. **Choose presence over clarity:** Rather than demanding answers, focus on staying present. Breathe. Walk. Rest. Eat. Do the next right thing. Show up to your life, even when it's uncertain.
3. **Lean into process, not outcomes:** Healing and understanding are not events—they are journeys. Embrace the small steps, and trust that clarity can emerge over time.
4. **Surround yourself with people who won't rush your pain:** You don't need quick fixes. You need slow, steady, patient presence. Seek out relationships where you're allowed to be in process.
5. **Practice spiritual honesty:** You can talk to God even

when you're angry or confused. You don't have to pretend. Honesty is the foundation of intimacy.

Job teaches us that silence is not always absence. Sometimes, it's the sacred ground where deeper truths are born. When answers don't come, we grow in other ways—in resilience, humility, and depth.

Honouring the Search

Too often, we downplay the search itself, treating it as something to rush through in pursuit of closure, but Job's journey reminds us that searching deserves its kind of reverence. It is sacred not to know. It is brave to keep seeking when no one guarantees you'll find what you want.

Job didn't abandon the search when answers didn't come. He kept asking, kept reflecting, kept reaching beyond his pain. And in that reaching, he honoured his humanity.

To search is to admit that something inside you still believes meaning exists. That even in the confusion, there's something worth uncovering. It is not weakness to ask, it's evidence of endurance.

We live in a world that celebrates certainty. People want clear answers, black-and-white categories, and fast resolutions, but growth happens in the grey, in the in-between, in the fog of questions and the slow uncovering of truth.

Honouring the search means allowing yourself to:

- **Ask without shame:** Even if your questions make others uncomfortable.
- **Sit in uncertainty:** Even if no resolution is in sight.
- **Feel without needing to fix:** Even if the pain feels pointless for now.
- **Trust your process:** Even if others think you're taking too long to move on.

Not every question leads to a clear answer, but every honest question deepens one's understanding of oneself and the world.
Job's search wasn't linear. It was messy. Emotional. Conflicted. But it was real. And that realness was its form of worship.

When we ask hard questions, we are not stepping away from faith; we walk deeper into it. Faith does not pretend to have all the answers. Faith trusts that we are still being led, even in the dark. So, if you are searching, keep going. There is something sacred in your pursuit.

Clues Hidden in the Ruins

When everything falls apart, it's easy to believe that nothing of value remains. The house is gone. The plans are shattered. The laughter has stopped. And all that's left are ashes. But sometimes, it's in those ashes that the first clues of transformation begin to emerge.

For Job, clarity wasn't wrapped in divine thunder or immediate answers. It came slowly. Quietly. In moments of deep lament. In reflections. He couldn't stop asking the questions. Clarity began as glimpses; small insights, flickers of wisdom, grains of understanding that pointed toward something deeper than the suffering itself.

In every season of loss, there are clues; truths that surface not despite the pain, but because of it. We don't always recognize them immediately, but they wait to be seen.

Here are some of the clues often hidden in the ruins:

1. **Revealed Priorities:** Loss has a way of stripping us down to what matters. In Job's case, it wasn't the animals or the property that left the deepest wound, it was the loss of his children, the isolation of his soul, and the silence of his God. Pain clarifies what comfort often clouds. What matters most becomes glaringly apparent when everything else is gone.
2. **Unexpected Resilience**: We often don't know how

strong we are until we have no choice but to be. Job didn't set out to become an example of endurance, but something solid within him remained as his world crumbled. His refusal to curse, his insistence on engaging, even when confused, proved that his spirit could withstand more than he thought.

3. **The True Nature of Relationships**: Crisis reveals character. Job's losses exposed the limitations of his friendships. It was painful but also clarified who could walk with him through fire and who couldn't. Sometimes it's only in the breaking that we see who's truly meant to build with us.

4. **Inner Voice Development**: In the noise of abundance, our inner voice can get drowned out, but in the silence of loss, it grows louder. Job found his voice in the ruins. A voice that questioned, challenged, and eventually paved the way for deeper truth. Pain sharpened his self-awareness.

5. **Shift from Performance to Presence**: Before the fall, Job was a man of great works, sacrifices, intercessions, and honourable living. After the collapse, he became a man of presence, deeply engaged with his emotions, vulnerable in his questioning, and real in his faith. He moved from doing to being. And sometimes, that's where the true growth happens.

6. **Seeds of Empathy:** There's something about loss that softens the heart. Though Job was already wise, his

suffering shaped him into someone who would later pray for those who had wounded him. That kind of empathy doesn't grow in comfort, it is cultivated in suffering.

These clues don't erase the pain or explain away the loss, but they help us understand that something can still be gained, even when everything seems gone.

Meaning doesn't always announce itself. Sometimes, it waits quietly in the corners of your brokenness, waiting for your eyes to adjust to the dark.

Job didn't find the answers he sought, not at first, but he did find something else: he found himself, and in finding himself, he began to make sense of the suffering.

Letting Purpose Emerge

There comes a point in every journey through pain when something subtle begins to shift. The questions don't disappear, and the ache doesn't vanish, but the posture changes. You stop demanding answers and start becoming present.

For Job, this shift was gradual. He didn't suddenly wake up with a revelation. But as his words poured out and the echoes of his anguish settled, something began to rise within him. He wasn't just crying out anymore, he was listening. Not to the opinions of his friends. Not to the silence of God. But to the deep stirrings within his soul.

This is often how purpose emerges, not as a booming voice or a shining light, but as a quiet conviction. A whisper that says: There's still something worth living for. Something to grow from. Something that can be built even from this.

Pain clears the clutter. It silences the noise. And in that stillness, we can finally hear what's been waiting to speak.

So, how can you begin identifying these quiet signs of purpose?

1. **Notice what still matters:** After everything falls apart, what values remain? What relationships feel worth fighting for? What truths feel more rooted than before? These are the seeds of purpose.

2. **Pay attention to what draws you:** It might be writing, talking, creating, or helping. Even in sorrow, some activities feel life-giving. They're not distractions, they're clues. Follow them gently.

3. **Identify how the pain is changing you:** Are you more patient? More honest? More empathetic? Pain doesn't only break, it shapes. Purpose often grows from the kind of person pain helps you become.

4. **Don't rush the meaning:** You don't have to name your purpose right away. You just have to stay open to it. Purpose unfolds, and when it's real, it fits quietly and

deeply.

5. **Make room for mystery:** Some aspects of your story may never be explained, but that doesn't mean they're useless. Purpose includes what you understand and choose to carry with grace.

Job's story doesn't tie up all the loose ends here, but it does begin to shift. Once desperate for clarity, the man starts to settle into deeper awareness. He hasn't stopped searching but is no longer searching for quick answers. He's searching for alignment, honesty, and peace.

As this chapter closes, consider your journey. What if you didn't need to understand everything to move forward? What if the search itself is shaping something sacred within you?

Pain is an influential teacher, but only when we stay long enough to listen.

In my distress,
I search for peace,
not around me, but
within.

chapter four
Managing Inner Turmoil

The Quiet Chaos Within

It's easy to look at Job's story and focus on what happened to him externally; his wealth gone, his children buried, his health shattered, but beneath the surface of those visible losses was a storm that no one could see. The real battle wasn't just around him. It was raging inside him.

Pain has a way of invading every layer of a person. It doesn't knock at the door politely. It tears through the front of the house and sets up camp in your chest, thoughts, and soul. And that's precisely where Job found himself, not just grieving the external world he'd lost, but wrestling with the quiet chaos within.

From the end of the earth will I cry unto thee, when my heart is overwhelmed: lead me to the rock that is higher than I.
Psalm 61:2

He was a man undone. His once clear mind was now crowded with confusion. His emotions, once anchored in a life of integrity and peace, were now violently tossed between hope and despair. Worst of all, the isolation meant no one could see it clearly because inner turmoil is often invisible to the outside world.

Within him was grief, not just for the lives lost, but for the life he no longer recognized.

There was anger, not the loud, uncontrollable kind, but the silent, simmering rage that arises when justice feels distant and life no longer makes sense; the anger of a man who had lived righteously, only to be struck by tragedy.

There was confusion, a mental fog that clouded what he once knew. The questions wouldn't stop, and the memories hurt to revisit. Everything he thought he understood about life, fairness, and faith was dismantled.

There was despair, a slow, suffocating weight that pressed on his chest daily. Not the dramatic kind seen in movies, but the kind that makes getting out of bed feel pointless. The kind that whispers, "This will never get better."

There was silence on the outside and the inside. The stillness of those who didn't understand, and the paralyzing quiet of a heart too wounded to speak clearly.

Why art thou cast down, O my soul?
and why art thou disquieted in me? hope thou
in God: for I shall yet praise him for the help
of his countenance.
Psalm 42:5

These emotions don't take turns. They don't show up neatly, one at a time. They cohabitate. They overlap. They come in waves, sometimes crashing, creeping.

If you've ever sat in your room unable to cry, not because you didn't feel anything, but because you thought about everything, you've been where Job was.

If you've ever stood in a crowd and felt utterly alone, if you've ever smiled for the world while screaming inside, if you've ever wondered, "What's wrong with me?" but couldn't put your finger on it; you know is a storm.

Internal chaos is not weakness. It is the natural fallout of profound loss. The deeper the attachment, the more violent the emotional aftermath. Yet many suffer silently, believing they must hold themselves together because others don't see the cracks.

Job shows us that the soul can break loudly, even if the

mouth doesn't. That internal storms are real. And that naming the chaos is the first act of reclaiming peace.

Naming the Storm

You can't fight what you can't see, and you can't heal what you won't name. That's the cruel trick of emotional pain. It often hides behind silence, shame, or exhaustion, but when you name it, you bring it into the light. You give it shape. You begin to take back control.

Job didn't use clinical language. He didn't sit with a therapist and chart his emotional state. But in his raw, poetic cries, he named what he felt, and in doing so, he permitted us to do the same.

Let's look at some of the layers of inner turmoil Job experienced, layers that many readers will recognize in themselves.

Grief over What's Lost

This ache hits you when the absence of something or someone becomes louder than their presence ever was. It's the echo of laughter that won't return, the empty chair at the table, the silence where joy used to live. Job grieved not just the loss of his children and possessions but the loss of the man he was before it all happened.

Fear of What's Ahead

When everything crumbles, the future becomes a fog. How do you rebuild when the foundation is gone? What if the worst isn't over? Job feared that more suffering might be ahead, that he might never be whole again. This fear paralyzes progress, making each step feel unsure.

Guilt over What Can't Be Undone

Even when we're not to blame, suffering stirs guilt. Did I miss a sign? Could I have prevented this? Did I fail them? Guilt is a thief. It steals clarity. It rewrites memory, and even in his righteousness, Job searched his past for something he might've done wrong. That's the pull of guilt; it doesn't wait for truth. It just accuses.

Anger at people—or God

Anger is the loudest and often the most misunderstood emotion. It's not always violent. Sometimes it simmers. Sometimes it cries. Sometimes it isolates. Job's anger wasn't just at his friends. It was directed toward the heavens. Why me? Why this? Anger, when unspoken, festers, but when named, it can lead to clarity and even reconciliation.

Loneliness in their Pain

Suffering often brings isolation, not because people don't care, but because they don't understand. Job was surrounded yet alone. Presence without empathy only sharpens loneliness, and the loneliest pain is the kind that others can't, or won't, see.

Numbness from Exhaustion

Then there's the silence that comes after the storm. The moments when you feel nothing at all. Not because you're okay, but because your soul is too tired to feel. Numbness isn't peace, it's pause. And Job had moments where he didn't have words, only ashes.

Naming emotions doesn't fix everything, but it's the first act of healing.
When you say, I am grieving, you stop pretending. When you admit, I am afraid, you invite comfort. When you confess, I am angry, you unravel what's beneath.

Pain thrives in secrecy. But the moment you name it, you start to own it, not as a sentence, but as a story, and stories can evolve. So take a moment. Look inward. What's stirring beneath the surface?

Call it out. Give it a name. And know that in doing so, you're not breaking, you're beginning.

The War Between Faith and Feelings

There's a battlefield many never speak of, the one between what we believe and feel. Job stood in the middle of that battlefield, torn between his convictions and condition. His faith told him that God is just, faithful, and present. His feelings screamed that life was unfair, God was silent, and pain had the final word.

This tension is not unique to Job. It is the quiet war waged in the hearts of countless people every day; those who believe in something greater but can't reconcile it with what they're going through.

Job had served faithfully, honoured God, lived righteously, and pursued a life of wisdom and humility. And yet, his world collapsed. As the losses mounted and the silence stretched, his emotions surged. He wept, questioned, raged, and doubted. And still, he kept talking to God.
This is the power of emotional honesty.

So many people carry guilt, not just for what they've done but for what they feel, for being sad too long, for being angry at God, for being numb when they think they should be grateful. They fear that expressing these things makes them weak, unfaithful, or broken beyond repair.

Here's the truth: emotional honesty is not rebellion. It's not faithlessness. It's intimacy.

To question is to care. To cry out is to connect. To feel deeply, even contradicting beliefs, is to be fully human.

Faith was never designed to suppress emotion. It was designed to carry it. To give it somewhere safe to land. Faith says, even when I don't understand, I'll stay in the conversation. That's what Job did.

He didn't hide his grief to protect God's reputation. He didn't silence his frustration to appear righteous. He laid it bare, unfiltered, unedited, and uncensored.

And in doing so, he taught us something sacred: that God can handle our honesty.

This war between faith and feelings isn't meant to be won. It's meant to be walked. It's where the most profound faith is formed, not in certainty, but in the willingness to show up with everything you carry.

If you've ever felt guilty for your emotions, let this be your permission to lay them down without shame. You can be angry and faithful. You can be confused and committed.

You can grieve and still believe.

Your feelings are not failures. They are signals. They can guide you toward deeper understanding, healing, and connection when listened to. Let them speak, let them breathe, and let them be heard. God isn't asking for performance. He's asking for presence.

Practices for Inner Stability

While Job's story is ancient, the emotional aftermath of pain and loss is timeless. What he endured on the inside mirrors what many go through today, waves of anxiety, emotional fatigue, bursts of sorrow, and a constant search for peace. Stability doesn't always mean solving the pain. Sometimes, it means learning to stand while it still hurts.

Here are practical ways to manage inner chaos; tools and rhythms that bring structure to emotional storms:

1. **Journaling Raw Thoughts Without Editing:** Writing is one of the most powerful ways to untangle what you feel. You don't need structure, grammar, or eloquence, just honesty. When you journal without censoring, you give your emotions a safe place to land. Over time, the page becomes a mirror, showing you growth, patterns, and prayers you didn't know were forming.
2. **Breathwork and Stillness Routines:** When in pain,

our bodies often tense up, mirroring the stress in our minds. Breathwork helps regulate your nervous system, grounding you in the present. Daily, a few minutes of deep, mindful breathing can reduce anxiety, clear mental fog, and reconnect you to your body. Pair this with silence, just sitting with yourself, and you'll start to feel your centre again.

3. **Seeking Professional or Pastoral Counselling**: You don't have to process everything alone. A therapist, counsellor, or spiritual advisor can provide perspective, validation, and guidance. Counselling offers language for emotions and a strategy for coping. Sometimes the breakthrough you need begins by simply being heard by someone trained to walk with you.

4. **Daily Affirmations Rooted in Truth and Grace**: The voice in your head can be your most prominent critic or your most outstanding support. Replace self-condemnation with affirmations that are gentle, true, and healing.

   Examples:

   - "I'm allowed to feel without fixing."
   - "I'm not my worst day."
   - "I am healing, even if slowly." Write them on mirrors.

   Say them out loud. Let them rewire the way you see yourself.

5. **Letting Go of the Need to Always 'Be Strong'**: True strength is not the absence of tears or fear; it's the courage to face them. You don't need to hold it together all the time. You're allowed to fall apart and rebuild. When you release the pressure to perform, you give yourself the gift of authenticity. Healing begins there.

6. **Creating Rhythms of Rest**: When your world falls apart, basic routines become anchors. Go to bed at a regular time. Eat nourishing food. Take short walks. Drink water. Grief and turmoil drain the body; rest restores it. Build rhythms that honour your humanity.

7. **Expressing Emotion Creatively:** Pain doesn't always exist through words. Sometimes it comes through painting, singing, cooking, or movement. Find an outlet that allows your emotions to flow without explaining them. Creativity makes space for healing in ways logic cannot.

8. **Limit Exposure to Emotional Triggers:** Guard your emotional energy. Step back if certain people, media, or environments escalate your inner chaos. It's okay to curate your input while you recover. Boundaries are not selfish; they're survival.

9. **Practice Gratitude Without Denial:** Gratitude and grief can coexist. You're not ignoring pain by naming what's still good. Whether it's the warmth of sunlight, laughter, or a moment of stillness, train your eyes to spot the minor signs of life. They don't cancel the pain, but they

soften it.

These practices won't remove the storm, but will help you build a shelter inside it.

Stability isn't about never feeling overwhelmed. It's about having a way back to your centre when you do.

How to Hold Hope and Hurt Together

Hope and hurt often seem like opposites, one light and the other dark. But in reality, they usually live in the same space. The deepest kind of resilience comes not from denying but from learning how to hold both.

Job was hurting, beyond words, beyond reason, beyond comfort. And yet, even in his anguish, something tethered him to a greater possibility. He wasn't cheerful. He wasn't pretending, but neither was he fully crushed. He lived in the tension, where pain screams and hope whispers.

Many people find themselves in this situation: grieving what's been lost but still holding onto something, maybe fragile, maybe flickering, that says, "There has to be more than this."

So, how do you live in that space?

1. **Accept the Coexistence:** You can be hopeful and heartbroken. You can believe in better days while mourning the present ones. Stop choosing between hope and hurt; acknowledge that both are valid and often simultaneous. This frees you from guilt when joy appears during grief or sadness lingers during a hopeful moment.

2. **Normalize the Emotional Tension:** Tears and trust can live side by side. Some days, hope will feel strong. Other days, pain will feel louder. That doesn't mean you're doing something wrong. It means you're human. Let your emotions move. Let your faith flex.

3. **Keep a Record of Small Graces:** During painful seasons, minor signs of progress can anchor you. Write down moments when you felt peace. When someone encouraged you. When your breath slowed. When you laughed, even briefly. These are the footprints of hope walking alongside your hurt.

4. **Avoid Toxic Positivity:** You don't have to smile through everything. You don't have to make your pain palatable for others. True hope doesn't dismiss pain, it honours it. Stay honest. Hope that requires denial isn't real hope. It's an escape.

5. **Speak Hope Even When You Don't Feel It:** There's power in declaring what you long for. Say it: "I will not feel like this forever." "I don't know how, but I believe healing is possible." These aren't lies; they're lifelines. Your words

can lead the way even if your heart hasn't caught up.

6. **Lean on Borrowed Hope:** When your hope feels too small, lean on someone else's. Let a friend's encouragement hold you up. Let a story inspire you. Let others carry what you can't. We're not meant to carry everything alone.

Hope doesn't eliminate hurt. It sits with it, softening its sharp edges and making space for new beginnings.

Job never claimed to be fine. But he did keep speaking. He stayed present in his process. And that quiet persistence is the greatest form of hope. You don't have to feel hopeful to be hopeful. You just have to show up. Again. And again. And again.

Transforming Inner Turmoil into Growth

Pain often feels like the end of the story. Imagining anything beautiful being birthed from it is hard when we're in emotional chaos, but Job's journey teaches us something different, something powerful. Inner turmoil is not just something to survive. It can be the soil where transformation takes root.

Job's suffering didn't make him weaker. It made him more aware, honest, and tuned in to what mattered. His cries into the silence became a spiritual excavation, uncovering parts of himself that success had buried. His grief opened the door to wisdom. His doubt led to deeper understanding.

His anger created space for authentic dialogue.

This gift is hidden in pain: when faced, felt, and processed, it becomes a tool, not just a wound.

1. **Growth Starts with Permission:** You don't need to be fully healed to start growing. You just need permission to feel, question, and evolve. Job didn't wait until he had answers. He grew in the middle of his asking.
2. **Emotional Awareness Builds Emotional Resilience:** By naming his grief, anger, fear, and confusion, Job became more emotionally intelligent. That self-awareness gave him strength. His feelings didn't control him, but he didn't deny them either. This balance is key to resilience.
3. **Struggle Clarifies Values:** In turmoil, what doesn't matter falls away. What remains is raw and real. Pain has a way of spotlighting your deepest beliefs. It refines your character, your integrity, and your purpose. What used to seem important may fade. What truly matters becomes clear.
4. **Pain Creates Pathways to Empathy:** Job once prayed for his children daily; he later prayed for his misguided friends. Why? Pain widened his heart. The kind of growth born from struggle is the kind that allows us to walk more gently through the world.
5. **Inner Turmoil Fuels Spiritual Depth:** Before the storm, Job had a reputation for being blameless and upright, but after the turmoil, he spoke more freely, personally,

and intimately with God. The wrestling deepened the relationship. He no longer knew about God—he knew Him.

Growth doesn't require perfection. It involves participation, showing up to your pain, sitting with your mess, listening to your inner voice, and being willing to let the experience shape, not shatter, you.

If you're in a storm of inner chaos right now, know this: the fact that you're still here, still searching, still reading, is proof that something inside you is growing even if you can't feel it yet.

The winds may not have stopped, and the tears may still fall, but something has shifted. You are no longer just surviving the storm but learning to transform in it.

Weeping may linger through the night, but something stirs by morning

chapter five
Glimpses of Hope

The First Flickers After the Dark

Job was still sitting in ashes. His body still bore the marks of pain. His world, by all accounts, had not changed. Yet something was shifting. Not around him, but within. It wasn't restoration, not yet. It wasn't joy, not entirely, but it was the first flicker of something fragile and new.

Hope rarely comes with a shout. It doesn't march into the room waving banners or announce itself with grand gestures. It arrives quietly; a thought, a breath, a pause in the grief, a brief reminder of something good, the ability to look up for a moment and imagine that things might not stay broken forever.

For Job, that flicker might have been found in his continued conversation. His still speaking, questioning, and wrestling showed that something in him hadn't given up. That, though the night was long, he hadn't surrendered to the darkness.

This is what the first flickers of hope often look like:

- The moment you feel the warmth of sunlight and acknowledge it.
- The first time you sleep through the night since the loss.
- A conversation that doesn't feel forced.
- Laughter that surprises you, because you didn't expect it.
- A sudden surge of energy that makes you want to clean, cook, or call someone.
- The thought: Maybe I'll be okay, even if tears follow it.

These moments might feel small. Insignificant. But they are not. They are the first signals that life is returning. That your heart, though battered, is still beating with intention. That healing doesn't start with a miracle, it begins with noticing.

The challenge is not whether hope appears. It's whether we recognize it when it does.

So pause, look around, look within, and ask yourself:

- What small thing lifted my spirit today?
- What didn't hurt as much as it did yesterday?
- What did I do that felt like movement, no matter how minor?

These are your flickers.
Don't dismiss them. Nurture them. Speak to them aloud. Write them down. Let them remind you that this painful chapter does not end in despair. Even in Job's ashes, a spark was rising. So, it is with you.

The Power of One Encouraging Thought

Sometimes, the only thing separating despair from hope is a single thought, a line of truth, a memory, a word of encouragement. It doesn't need to be profound or poetic. It just needs to be real.

For Job, that shift might have begun with realizing he was still here. That, though everything around him had collapsed, he hadn't. He was broken but breathing. That mattered.

One encouraging thought can change the entire trajectory of the mind. It doesn't erase the pain, but it repositions it. It reminds us that while we cannot control the storm, we can decide where to stand.

The human mind is mighty, capable of directing how we see, feel, and respond to our reality. What we focus on shapes what we believe. And what we believe determines what we do next. Even when the body is weary, the mind

can begin to stir. And as it stirs, it starts to lead.
Hope doesn't wait for circumstances to change. It often shows up before the breakthrough. It starts in the mind as a whisper of possibility. From there, it travels to the heart, the body, and eventually, to our actions.

Consider these micro-moments of hope:

- You remember something you once loved and want to try again.
- A friend sends a message, and you smile for the first time in days.
- You hear someone's story of survival, and something inside you whispers, "Maybe me too."
- You wake up without dreading the day.
- You clean one corner of a room and feel a spark of control return.
- You pray, not because you have the words, but because you want to believe they matter.

These aren't miracles in the dramatic sense. They are miracles of the mind, the kind that begin the rebuilding before the evidence shows up.

Encouragement doesn't always have to come from outside. Sometimes it begins within. Your voice says, "I've been through worse." "I'm still needed." "This isn't the end of me."

The atmosphere inside you shifts, not because life is

suddenly perfect, but because your thoughts are no longer surrendering to defeat. So take note of every flicker, every moment when you feel even slightly more alive than the day before. That's not accidental. That's hope finding a foothold.

Recognizing Signs of Life Within

Not all healing begins with grand gestures. Most of it doesn't. It starts with whispers, faint signals that your heart, mind, and spirit are slowly starting to stir again. After the depths of despair, these signs can feel so small that you might miss them, but they are worth noticing. They are signs of life within.

For Job, it didn't start with restoring wealth or reputation. It began with his willingness to speak again. To question. To stay present in his pain rather than withdraw completely. That was a sign of life.

Here are some ways you can begin to recognize their signs of internal resurrection:

1. **Curiosity Returns:** You find yourself wondering about something beyond your pain. Maybe it's a book you want to read. A place you want to visit. A question you want answered. Curiosity is the brain's way of saying, I still want to engage with the world.
2. **Desire to Connect Again:** You feel a nudge to reach out

to someone, not out of obligation, but because part of you misses a connection. Maybe it's a text you send. A comment you leave. A coffee date you finally say yes to. This desire is a sign that isolation is beginning to lift.

3. **Strength to Speak:** Your voice returns, not just the physical ability to talk, but the courage to share your feelings. To tell your story. To say, "I'm not okay" or "I'm trying." Speaking is a declaration that your inner world matters.
4. **Willingness to Try:** You take a walk. You tidy a room. You sign up for something. It may feel small, but effort is energy. Trying again, at anything, is a marker of movement.
5. **Feeling Something Again:** Even if the feelings are mixed, such as joy, nostalgia, sadness, or comfort, the fact that you are feeling again is significant. Numbness is the absence of emotional movement. Emotion, even if painful, signals you're alive inside.
6. **Re-engaging with Routine:** You begin to crave rhythm. A regular wake time. A meal you enjoy preparing. Small habits that root you back in the flow of life. Routine provides safety; seeking it out is a subconscious way of choosing stability.
7. **Hopeful Imagination:** You catch yourself daydreaming. You envision the future, even vaguely. You picture something beyond the valley. Imagination is not escapism here, it's forward movement.
8. **Feeling Protective of Your Progress:** You notice yourself setting boundaries, turning down negativity, or avoiding what drains you. This protectiveness is a sign that you

value your healing, even if it's fragile.

Tips to Help You Notice These Signs:

- **Reflect Daily:** Ask, "What felt different today?" or "Where did I feel most alive?"
- **Keep a 'Hope Journal':** Write down even the smallest signs of progress, no matter how minor they seem.
- **Celebrate Micro-wins:** Treat small victories like breakthroughs. That walk, that laugh, that moment of peace, they matter.
- **Share Your Observations:** Talk to someone about what you're noticing. Their feedback may reveal even more growth than you can see.
- **Don't Compare:** Healing isn't linear. Your pace is your own. Celebrate it without judgment.

Recognizing these signs helps you reclaim your agency. It reminds you that healing is not something that happens to you. It's something that happens in you, and it's happening, even now.

Learning to Breathe Again

After the shock of loss, it's common to forget how to breathe. Not physically, of course, our lungs keep working, but emotionally, spiritually, mentally. Everything feels constricted. Every breath feels shallow. Fear, sadness, and numbness sit heavy on the chest.

For Job, his breath was once so strong that it upheld his household, but in his grief, that breath faltered. There were moments he wished it had stopped altogether. Yet, with time, breath returned, not as a roar, but as a quiet rhythm.

To learn to breathe again is to return to life, slowly, intentionally, and gently. Here's what It means to breathe again:

- **You pause before reacting.** This moment of stillness is the beginning of mindfulness, a sign that your soul is beginning to settle.
- **You feel your shoulders drop.** The tension in your body for weeks or months begins to release, even if just a little. That release is progress.
- **You begin to rest, not just sleep.** Your nights are not all peaceful, but you notice one where your body truly feels safe enough to recharge.
- **You exhale without fear.** This feels like letting go of a burden, making a decision, saying a hard truth, breathing through discomfort instead of holding your breath against it.

Why This Matters:

Breathing is foundational. It affects everything: your focus, your sleep, your energy, and your emotions. When you relearn how to breathe with intention, you create space inside yourself for healing, clarity, and calm.

Practical Ways to Breathe Again:

- **Breathwork practice:** Try inhaling for four seconds, holding for four, and exhaling for six. Repeat this for a few minutes each morning or when overwhelmed.
- **Stretch and move:** Gentle stretching, yoga, or walking outdoors opens your chest and invites air into the places where grief has settled.
- **Silence breaks:** Once a day, sit in stillness with closed eyes and simply breathe. No phone, no agenda, just breathe.
- **Name what's heavy, then exhale:** Imagine releasing what's been sitting in your chest as you breathe. Grief. Anger. Shame. It may not disappear, but it begins to lose its grip.
- **Anchor to the moment:** Use your breath to ground yourself. "I am here. I am breathing. I am okay for this moment." That's often enough.

Breathing again is not the end of grief but often the beginning of peace. Each breath is a vote for life. A quiet way of saying, "I'm still here." And with each inhale, hope expands just a little more.

Building on the Small Wins

After an intense emotional or spiritual collapse, it's easy to believe that only big gestures can prove healing has begun. But the reality is that rebuilding doesn't start with leaps. It starts with steps, small ones, repetitive ones, quiet ones, and every step matters.

For Job, we don't see immediate transformation. We see a slow, gritty return to presence. His wins weren't dramatic; they were deeply human: staying in the conversation, enduring the silence, not abandoning his soul's questions. Those were victories.

If you're emerging from your storm, now is the time to focus on and build on your small wins.

What Small Wins Look Like:

- You walk not because you must, but because you want to feel the sun.
- You write down one sentence about how you feel today.
- You reply to a message you ignored for weeks.
- You choose a nourishing meal over skipping food.
- You say 'yes' to one life-giving thing.
- You let yourself laugh and don't apologize for it.

These are not minor. These are markers. Each one is a piece of you returning home to yourself. Here is a working process for rebuilding:

1. **Notice**: Pay attention to what feels like growth. Don't judge it. Just name it.
2. **Nurture**: Once you see it, care for it. Water it with repetition. Show up for it daily, even when it's small.
3. **Record:** Keep track of your wins. Use a simple notebook, voice note, or daily reflection. This will build confidence.
4. **Share:** Let someone know—a friend, mentor, or therapist. Speaking your growth solidifies it.
5. **Reinforce**: add to it. Stack one positive step on top of another. Let the momentum build naturally.

Healing thrives in gentle consistency.

Whether walking, journaling, re-engaging in prayer, or reconnecting with people slowly, each step you take toward wholeness is significant. Even if we've touched on these earlier, each appearance is a fresh application. In Job's case, it wasn't about novelty, it was about persistence.

You don't need a perfect plan. You need the courage to take one more step than you did yesterday. The story is not done. The rebuilding has begun.

What Hope Does, Even If Circumstances Haven't Changed

Hope is not wishful thinking. It's not naiveté or denial. Hope is a forward-facing, soul-level strength that dares to look pain in the eye and say, "You will not define my entire story." Hope doesn't mean everything's okay; it means you believe that someday, things could be.

When everything around you feels static, when the diagnosis hasn't changed, the loss is still real, the relationship remains strained, hope is what shifts you. And that shift, even if subtle, is everything.

Although the fig tree shall not blossom,
neither shall fruit be in the vines; the labour of the olive
shall fail, and the fields shall yield no meat; the flock shall
be cut off from the fold, and there shall be no herd in the
stalls: Yet I will rejoice in the LORD, I will joy in the
God of my salvation.

Habakkuk 3:17-18

---

1. Hope Lifts Perspective: Pain pulls your gaze downward, narrowing your focus to what's broken, missing, and wrong, but hope lifts your eyes, maybe not all the way, but just enough to see beyond the immediate. It whispers, "This isn't all there is."

Even when Job still had nothing materially restored, he shifted inwardly. He started speaking from deeper places.

His questions weren't just desperate, they were reflective. That shift didn't fix his problems. But it changed his position. He wasn't lying in the dust anymore, he was looking up.

Perspective is power. It doesn't eliminate pain, but it allows you to reframe it. To see it as part of a larger narrative, not the end of one.

2. Hope Strengthens Endurance: Hope is fuel. It doesn't just get you through a day, it gets you through a season.

When you believe that healing could come, that change might arrive, that joy may return, you find strength you didn't know you had. You keep showing up. You keep breathing. You keep trying. Not because it's easy, but because something inside you believes the effort still matters.

Job's endurance wasn't rooted in denial; it was sustained by the quiet possibility that his pain wasn't meaningless. That endurance didn't eliminate his sorrow but kept him from giving up on it.

Endurance shaped by hope is not just survival. It's preparation. It's building capacity for what's coming, even when you can't yet see it.

3. Hope Awakens Vision: Without hope, you stop imagining. Your dreams shrivel. Your creativity dulls. Your future becomes a blank wall instead of a window.

When hope returns, even slightly, vision is reawakened. You begin to imagine again, maybe not with full detail, but with colour. You picture yourself laughing. Building. Loving. Living. That vision isn't delusion, it's direction. It gives you something to move toward.

Job didn't know what was coming, but something stirred in him. His dialogue evolved, and his insight deepened. He spoke not just as a man who suffered but as one who could see beyond the suffering. That shift in vision didn't change his circumstances, but it changed him.

4. Hope Grounds You When You Can't Control Anything Else: One of the most disorienting parts of suffering is the loss of control. You can't control the diagnosis, the departure, the disaster, but you can control your posture. Hope grounds you when your footing is unsure. It says, "I may not control the storm, but I can control how I stand in it."

Job may have lost everything, but he didn't lose his footing entirely. Hope kept him upright. When his friends misjudged him, and the heavens were silent, hope steadied his voice. It gave him words. It gave him breath. That's what hope does. It becomes an anchor when the waves threaten to sweep you away.

5. Hope Is a Rebellion against Despair: Despair tells you it's over. Hope argues back. Whenever you dare to dream, plan, try, or believe again, you rebel against the narrative that says you're finished. Job's speeches weren't polished. His faith was shaky, but his refusal to curse his future was a quiet, consistent rebellion. Even his questions were hopeful; they assumed that someone might be listening.

Whenever you choose to trust in the dark, you resist despair. Hope is not passive, it is defiant.

6. Hope Redefines the Story: Job's story didn't begin with hope. It started with loss, but as his journey unfolds, hope becomes a new thread, subtle at first, then bold. It reframes the pain. It doesn't justify it, but it gives it context. It says, "This chapter is not the conclusion."
Your story, too, might still feel incomplete. Hope doesn't erase what's happened. It gives meaning to what happens next. It helps you rewrite the second half with intention.

7. Hope Can Be Quiet and Still Be Real: Don't wait for dramatic feelings. Hope doesn't always feel like a fire. Sometimes, it's a spark. Sometimes it's a warm breath in cold air. Sometimes it's the decision to try again tomorrow.

Job's hope wasn't loud. It didn't come with certainty or confidence, but it came. And it stayed. You may still be sitting in the same place, circumstances untouched, prayers unanswered, but if there's a flicker of light in you, fan it. Let it grow. Hope won't change your past, but it will change your path.

Hope isn't always the loudest voice. In Job's story, it was rarely loud at all, but it was present. Beneath the rubble of loss, beneath the ash and the aching questions, something remained. Something waited, and when the time was right, it stirred.

You may still be sitting in your version of loss. The pain may still be raw. The answers may still be far. But if something in you has started to move, even slightly, you are not where you started.

This chapter wasn't about resolution. It was about recognition. That healing often comes quietly. That progress can look like breathing. That recovery can begin even when circumstances have not shifted.

Job's transformation didn't happen overnight. There was no magic word. No sudden rescue. It began when he stayed present in his life, even when he didn't understand it. He dared to speak, to question, to feel. And in doing so, he allowed the smallest sparks of life to re-enter the spaces where death had ruled.

As we turn to the next chapter, we enter the story's heart, the turning point not just in Job's situation, but in his spirit. Pain, when given space, can serve a purpose. Suffering, when held well, can become sacred.

Pain insists upon being attended to. God whispers in our pleasures, speaks in our conscience, but shouts in our pains.

– C.S. Lewis.

chapter six
From Pain to Purpose

When life fractures under the weight of grief, loss, or suffering, it's tempting to focus on survival alone. And sometimes, survival is enough. But buried beneath even our worst seasons lies a deeper invitation, an opportunity to reach for purpose not as a distraction or fast-track to closure but as a compass.

Purpose doesn't cancel out pain. It doesn't deny the grief or speed up the process but gives pain a destination. It provides something to hold onto when everything else has been stripped away.

Job didn't set out to find purpose, he set out to find answers. To make sense of chaos. Yet purpose began to form somewhere along the way, between the ashes, the silence, and the long conversations with misguided friends. It didn't arrive with clarity. It emerged slowly, shaped by experience, deepened through reflection, and clarified by perseverance.

That's why we're using the word PURPOSE to frame this chapter. Not as a slogan, but as a structure. A way to explore how even the most shattered parts of life can become sacred ground for meaning.

Let's Begin with the First Step in the Journey

P – Persevere Through the Trial: Job endured what few of us could imagine. The collapse wasn't only financial or physical. It was emotional, relational, and spiritual. He lost his children, wealth, health, reputation, sense of stability, and perhaps worst of all, sense of divine nearness, and yet he remained.

There were no fireworks in his perseverance, no speeches of triumph, and no crowds applauding. He simply woke up and faced another day of pain. He stayed present to his questions, kept breathing, didn't curse God, or numb himself into silence. His perseverance didn't look heroic; it looked human.

That's the truth about endurance: it rarely feels powerful. More often, it feels like getting out of bed when your soul is too heavy. It feels like showing up to a world that no

longer makes sense. It's the quiet act of not giving up, not because you feel strong, but because something in you refuses to vanish.
Job's perseverance was raw and unfiltered. He didn't pretend to be okay. He voiced his despair. He sat in ashes. He wished for death. But he never disengaged. His pain drove him deeper, not away.

To persevere is not to smile through suffering. It is to stay. It's to let the pain be real while holding onto the thread of your existence. That thread may fray, but it's enough.
Your perseverance matters if you are in a season of your undoing, where everything is heavy and nothing seems stable. You may not feel noble or brave, but showing up counts.

Like Job, your silence might stretch long. Your prayers might feel unanswered, but the fact that you are still here, open, and searching is evidence of strength.

Perseverance is not the absence of suffering. It is the decision to stay in the story anyway.

U – Use the Pain for Progress: Pain is a terrible teacher, but it's often the most honest. It doesn't flatter. It doesn't coddle. It exposes what we've depended on, what we've ignored, and what we've believed without testing. And while pain is never something we seek, it becomes an opportunity for growth when we let it inform, not define us.

Job didn't rush to interpret his pain. He sat with it, talked through it, and listened even when others' words wounded him more than they healed, but in time, his suffering gave birth to new insight. His language changed, his perspective expanded, and his faith, though shaken, deepened.

Pain can shut us down or shake us awake. The choice is rarely evident in the moment, but when we begin to look at pain with intention, asking what it might reveal, challenge, or shift within us, we begin to progress.

Here's how pain can be used for progress:

- **It clarifies priorities.** What once consumed us, titles, wealth, status, often fades in urgency during pain. Job's identity was stripped down to its essence. In that nakedness, clarity emerged.
- **It stretches our empathy.** Suffering softens the heart. We become more aware of others, more patient, and more gracious. Job, who once offered sacrifices on behalf of his children, would later offer prayers for those who misjudged him. That arc, from pain to compassion, is progress.
- **It invites introspection.** Job began to ask deeper questions, not just about why bad things happen, but about the nature of justice, the voice of God, and the substance of life itself. Those questions shaped his soul.
- **It sparks transformation.** When processed with honesty,

pain changes us. It dismantles illusions, exposes character, and creates space for something new to grow.

Progress doesn't mean you're "over it." It means you're moving with it, not letting the pain sit idle and rot, but allowing it to push you toward something richer.

If you've suffered deeply, your progress may feel invisible, but if your perspective has widened, your heart has softened, or your questions have matured, pain has done its work. You're not just enduring the storm. You're evolving within it.

R – Realign with Meaning: Pain has a way of pulling us off course. When blindsided by tragedy, betrayal, or loss, we can become disoriented, unsure of who we are or what anything means. Our foundations are shaken. The beliefs we once held tightly seem to slip through our fingers. The routines that used to give our lives structure now feel empty or irrelevant.

This is where realignment becomes essential.

Realignment doesn't erase what happened. It helps us rediscover direction in the aftermath of impact. It's the gentle, difficult work of asking: What still matters? What do I now believe? Who am I, really, without the things I lost?

For Job, realignment didn't happen in a single moment.

It was the result of many conversations, many doubts, and many reflections. He began his journey consumed by questions: Why did this happen? What did I do wrong? Why has God abandoned me? Somewhere along the way, the "why" shifted toward what now?

He no longer demanded simple explanations. Instead, he began to explore deeper truths. He shifted from legalistic theology, I did good, so I should get good, to a more expansive view of mystery, grace, and humility. He began to see that purpose and peace don't always come from answers. Sometimes, they come from presence, staying engaged with your soul and questions.

How do we realign with meaning after pain?

- **Pause to Examine What You've Built Your Life On:** Loss tends to reveal what we've been leaning on. Whether it's success, relationships, health, or control, suffering shows us what can and cannot hold us. Realignment begins when we examine those structures and ask what deserves to remain.
- **Let Go of False Narratives:** Job had to release the idea that suffering is always punishment. Many of us must do the same, letting go of the belief that if bad things happen, we are to blame or that a life of faith guarantees comfort. These narratives are not only untrue—they are destructive.
- **Ask Better Questions:** Instead of asking, "Why is this happening to me?" try, "What is this revealing in me?"

Or, "What kind of person am I becoming in this process?" These questions don't have instant answers but lead to deeper awareness.

- **Rebuild Identity with Intention:** Now that things have changed, who are you? Who do you want to be going forward? Job could no longer be the father, leader, or friend he once was in the same way. But that didn't mean his story was over. It meant he had to write a new chapter, based on truth rather than assumption.
- **Redefine What Matters Most:** Suffering often simplifies things. We stop chasing everything and start noticing what's essential. Realignment is a return to what matters: relationships, peace, purpose, integrity, and hope. These become our new compass.

Realigning with meaning doesn't mean we stop grieving. It means we begin to grow roots again, this time, deeper. It means we start to live not in reaction to the pain, but in response to what the pain taught us.

You may not understand everything that happened. But you can choose to realign your life with what's meaningful now. With what's true now. With what still endures.

Pain will pull you off course, but meaning will bring you back.

P – Prepare for Renewal: After long seasons of grief or suffering, it's easy to believe that nothing good could ever emerge from the wreckage. The instinct is often to brace for more loss, not to anticipate restoration, but healing isn't just about survival. It's about readiness. Renewal rarely happens all at once. It begins with subtle signs, internal shifts, and the quiet work of preparing for what might be next.

Job didn't know renewal was on the horizon. His health hadn't returned, his relationships remained fractured, and his prayers were still unanswered, but something in his posture began to shift, not physically but spiritually. He started to lean forward again toward possibility, grace, and reconciliation. That's preparation.

What does preparing for renewal look like?

- **Letting Go of Bitterness:** Renewal cannot coexist with resentment. If your heart is still bound by what was done to you or what you lost, it's difficult to embrace anything new. Preparation begins with forgiveness, not because others deserve it, but because your future does.
- **Softening Your Defences:** Pain can harden us. We build walls to avoid more hurt, but those same walls can block the sunlight of healing. Preparing for renewal means softening, letting joy back in, even in small doses, and believing that goodness might find you again.
- **Restoring Inner Trust:** Trauma often makes us doubt ourselves. Preparing for renewal involves learning to trust your inner voice again, to believe your instincts,

honour your emotions, and permit yourself to want more from life.

- **Creating Space for the New:** Renewal requires room; room in your calendar, mind, and heart. This might mean releasing old expectations, relationships, or habits that no longer serve who you're becoming.
- **Surrendering the Timeline:** Job didn't know when, or if, restoration would come. He wasn't striving for it. He simply stayed open to it. Preparing for renewal isn't about chasing an outcome—it's about posturing your life to be ready for it if and when it arrives.
- **Beginning to Speak Differently:** Job's language slowly changed. He started asking different questions and speaking humbly, seeking understanding instead of control. Renewal is often preceded by a shift in voice—from anger to openness, from demanding to discerning.

Here are signs you're preparing for renewal (even If you don't realize it):

- You're starting to hope again, even cautiously.
- You're curious about your future, not just dreading it.
- You're willing to revisit relationships or goals you had given up on.
- You're less consumed with "why me?" and more drawn to "what now?"
- You're beginning to care for yourself in ways you previously ignored.

Preparing for renewal doesn't mean pretending the past didn't happen. It means accepting that while the pain shaped you, it doesn't have to define you.

Job's renewal began in spirit before it ever touched his circumstances. He was being readied for what he could not yet see. You may not see what's next, but your readiness matters. The next part of your story may not be restoration of what was, but the unveiling of something entirely new.

O – Offer Grace: Grace is difficult to offer, especially to those who have misjudged, misunderstood, or wounded us. Yet, as Job's journey nears its transformational peak, this is precisely what he does. He offers grace to the very people who added to his suffering.

When Job's friends came to "comfort" him, they condemned him. They made assumptions, questioned his integrity, and spoke from spiritual pride rather than genuine compassion. And yet, when God prepares to restore Job, one of the final acts required of him is to pray for these same friends.

It's a moment rich with symbolism. Job's healing is tied to his perseverance and willingness to extend grace.

What Does It Mean to Offer Grace?

- **It means releasing others from the debt of your pain:** Grace says, "You hurt me, but I will not let your actions define how I treat you." It is not forgetfulness, it's freedom. It's the refusal to let bitterness take root.

- **It's not agreement—it's surrender:** You don't have to approve of what was said or done. You simply decide that their offense will not be your identity. You lay it down, not for their benefit, but for your liberation.
- **It creates space for transformation—yours and theirs:** Job's prayer became a bridge, a sacred act that invited both accountability and healing. When we offer grace, we open the door for reconciliation—not always immediately, but eventually.
- **It reconnects us to purpose:** Carrying pain without grace distorts your focus, consumes emotional energy, and clouds your vision. Grace clarifies, resets the lens, and realigns you with what matters most.

How to Begin Offering Grace

- **Start with empathy.** Ask, what must have been happening for them to behave this way?
- **Speak your truth and then release it.** Write a letter, speak to a counsellor, or confide in a trusted friend. Don't bury your pain; process it honestly.
- **Pray for their good, even if it's difficult.** Like Job, this doesn't have to feel comfortable, but it breaks the hold their actions have on your heart.
- **Choose peace over proof.** You may never get an apology. You may never prove your innocence. Offer grace anyway. Not because they're right, but because

you want to be free.

Grace does not ignore justice. But it invites mercy into the conversation. And sometimes, healing cannot begin until grace has had the final word.

Job didn't get retribution. He got restoration. Not by demanding it, but by releasing others from what they owed him.

You may never receive closure from those who caused your pain, but you can still choose healing. And often, it starts with grace.

S – Stand with Resilience: Resilience isn't about bouncing back. It's about rising forward. It's not the act of returning to who you were before the pain; it's becoming someone stronger, deeper, and wiser because of it.

When Job stood again, he wasn't the same man who once walked in prosperity. He had been humbled, wounded, stripped bare. He had faced not only loss but silence, shame, and the suspicion of those closest to him. He had wrestled with his thoughts, shouted his frustrations to the sky, and waited without answers. Yet, somehow, he rose.

Not with triumphant certainty. Not with polished eloquence. But with resilience—the quiet strength that develops when you've endured what should have broken you.
What Does It Mean to Stand with Resilience?

- **It means standing while still scarred:** Resilience doesn't wait for the wound to vanish. It chooses to move forward even with the limp. It says I've been through the worst and am still here.
- **It means choosing life again, day by day:** After trauma or profound grief, even the most basic decisions like getting out of bed, eating well, and trying something new become acts of courage. Resilience isn't measured in grand gestures, but in these small but defiant daily choices.
- **It means owning your story without shame:** Job didn't hide what happened to him. He named it, lived it, and brought it to God. Standing with resilience means refusing to be defined by what happened to you but not denying it.
- **It means holding faith and uncertainty at once:** Resilience doesn't erase doubt, it makes space for it. Job's journey wasn't tidy. It was filled with questions and contradictions. Still, he chose to keep showing up. To stay in the conversation. To believe that the silence would break, and eventually, it did.
- **It means rebuilding, not from what was lost, but from what was learned:** What Job regained wasn't a carbon copy of his former life. It was something new. Restoration often comes in unfamiliar forms. Resilience accepts that. It builds forward, not backward.

How Do You Cultivate Resilience?

- **Allow yourself to rest but not to quit.** Rest is recovery, and quitting is resignation. Learn the difference.
- **Speak kindly to yourself.** The inner narrative shapes the outer journey. Resilient people learn to replace self-criticism with self-compassion.
- **Surround yourself with truth-tellers**. People who will walk with you, not just comfort or challenge you, but see you clearly and help you stay grounded.
- **Track your strength.** Write down moments when you acted with courage or clarity. Remind yourself: I've survived before. I will rise again.

Job stood resiliently, not because the world clapped for him but because he refused to collapse. He stood as someone changed but not destroyed, someone who no longer needed to have it all to know he was whole.

You are resilient if you are still standing after your storm, no matter how fragile you feel.

E – Emerge Transformed: Every journey through pain reshapes us, but not every person emerges from pain transformed. Some come out bitter, others numb, and others give up halfway. True transformation doesn't come automatically with time; it comes with intention, surrender, and reflection.

When Job emerged from his long valley of suffering, he

wasn't merely restored but transformed. He gained more than possessions, he gained perspective. He saw life, faith, people, and even himself differently. He became a man who had lived through agony, questioned everything, and still chose to walk forward.

Transformation isn't about returning to who you were. It's about becoming who you couldn't have been without the pain.

What Does Transformation Look Like?

- **Greater empathy and grace:** Job prayed for his friends, not out of duty, but because something had shifted in him. He had learned that everyone, even those who wound, often hurts themselves.
- **Wider vision:**Job's understanding of God was stretched. He saw a bigger picture that included mystery, paradox, and mercy. Transformation continually expands how we see.
- **Deeper identity:** Stripped of titles, roles, and reputation, Job found who he was at the core. That's what suffering does, it removes the surface so we can see the soul.
- **Humbled strength:** He wasn't triumphant in a worldly sense. He was grounded. Rooted. Sure. Transformation makes us quieter, not louder. Gentler, not weaker. Stronger, not harder.

What It Takes to Emerge Transformed

- **Reflection:** You must be willing to look back, not dwell, but learn.
- **Surrender:** Transformation doesn't come from control—it comes from trust.
- **Release:** You cannot carry old narratives and expect new beginnings.
- **Gratitude:** Even when life didn't go as expected, choosing gratitude changes how you carry the scars.

Transformation is not a return, it's a rebirth.

Job's story didn't end with answers. It ended with a revelation: a new way of seeing God, a more profound sense of self, a renewed relationship with others, and a testimony that would live long beyond his generation.

You may not understand all that you've walked through. But you can choose what kind of person you become because of it. Transformation is no longer a distant hope when pain becomes purpose and wounds become wisdom. It becomes your reality.

You're not just surviving. You're emerging changed, wiser, deeper.

The Purpose Beneath the Pain

Pain is not the end of the story. More often than not, it is the soil in which something far greater takes root.

When Job sat in silence, surrounded by ashes and the fragments of a once-full life, there was no sign that purpose remained. Yet, something was forming, not despite the pain but through it. Each cry, question, and breath in the dark carried him closer to a transformation he couldn't yet see.

That's how purpose often works. It doesn't appear as a blazing light or a perfect answer. It grows slowly. It lives beneath the surface. It works through broken pieces, and one day, without warning, it rises.

Pain stripped Job of everything the world said defined him, but what emerged in its place was someone wiser, softer, and more rooted than ever. Someone who knew what it meant to suffer, and what it meant to forgive. Someone who could look at the people who wounded him and pray for them. Someone who had wrestled with questions that never found answers and came out holding something better, truth, depth, perspective, and peace.

That is the purpose beneath the pain: to survive and become through it. To awaken parts of yourself that comfort never had the power to reach, to learn the language of compassion, to walk humbly with others, and to hold space for mystery.

And God sent me before you to preserve you a posterity in the earth, and to save your lives by a great deliverance. So now it was not you that sent me hither, but God: and he hath made me a father to Pharaoh, and lord of all his house, and a ruler throughout all the land of Egypt.

Genesis 45:7-8

You may not yet know what your pain will produce, but if you've made it this far, something is already growing in you. Keep walking. Keep breathing. Keep showing up.

What you lost may never be restored exactly the way it was, but what you gain. If you let the pain shape you—may be more beautiful, lasting, and meaningful than you ever imagined.

Forgiveness is not weakness. It is the power to rise above what tried to ruin you

chapter seven
Restorative Forgiveness

The Aftershock of Pain

There's a kind of pain that doesn't end when the event is over. It lingers, echoes, and lodges itself into memory and marrow long after the world has moved on. This is the aftershock, the emotional debris that refuses to clear just because time has passed.

For Job, the deepest wounds were not only from loss. They were from people. Friends who once walked with him, who sat with him in silence, eventually turned against him. Instead of comfort, they brought criticism. Instead of empathy, they offered accusations. They dissected his suffering and questioned his worth. And when the dust settled, the weight of their betrayal hung heavier than silence itself.

This is often the case with pain inflicted by those who should have protected us. The ones we leaned on become the ones we're forced to recover from. Their words sting longer. Their absence echoes louder. Their misunderstanding cuts deeper, and their judgment, often subtle, wounds the soul in ways we struggle to name.

Yet, in most cases, the world expects us to bounce back, smile again, and get over it. The calendar moves on. Responsibilities return. People, even those who hurt us, look at us as if to say, "You're still stuck there?" They may not mean harm, but the effect is still isolating. Their impatience with our healing can feel like a second betrayal.

That kind of pressure can be paralyzing. It occurs when you're grieving but expected to perform, when you're aching inside but must carry on like everything is fine, and when even the people closest to you act as though your silence means you're done hurting. Healing doesn't respond to pressure. It responds to the process.

Pain, especially relational pain, doesn't just dissolve with time. It must be addressed, acknowledged, and cleared out. It must be picked up piece by piece like shattered glass in a room, each shard carrying its memory and meaning.

Psychologically, this aftershock creates inner conflict. You begin to doubt your timeline. You wonder if you're being overly sensitive. You try to mask your feelings to avoid judgment, but every time you repress your grief, you distance yourself from recovery.

Job's healing didn't begin the moment his trials ended. It started when he made space for something else, when he cleared the emotional wreckage that had built up between him and his community. That meant first acknowledging that the pain was real, lingering, and heavy.

His story invites us to slow down. To listen to what still hurts, to name what hasn't yet healed, and to honour the grief that no one else sees.

You are not alone if you've ever felt like the world moved on while bleeding. The aftershock is valid. Your story deserves space to breathe. Forgiveness does not begin with forgetting. It starts with feeling.

The Weight of Bitterness

Unforgiveness is not passive. It is weighty. It latches onto our emotions and infiltrates our thoughts. It shows up in our conversations and shadows our interactions. Left unchecked, it doesn't just affect how we feel, it reshapes who we are becoming.

Job could have easily carried the burden of resentment, toward his friends for misrepresenting his heart, toward life, for being so suddenly and violently unravelled, and even toward God, for allowing such calamity without explanation.

Bitterness doesn't always announce itself. Sometimes, it hides behind sarcasm, withdrawal, an overprotective spirit, or a distrustful gaze, but eventually, it shows, and when it does, it steals joy, dims perspective, and isolates us from healing.

The Dangers of Unprocessed Anger and Bitterness:

1. **It hardens the heart:** When we rehearse pain without releasing it, our heart becomes less open to compassion and connection. What once was a defence becomes a prison.
2. **It distorts perception:** Bitterness alters how we see the world. We begin to anticipate harm even where there is none. It turns caution into cynicism.
3. **It poisons relationships:** Resentment doesn't stay confined. It seeps into how we speak, listen, and behave in relationships, often pushing away those who genuinely care.
4. **It traps us in the past:** Bitterness keeps the wound open. We replay the offense, relive the pain, and resist any attempt to move forward.
5. **It erodes self-worth:** When you hold onto what was done to you, your identity can become tethered to that moment. You begin to see yourself through the lens of the offense.
6. **It distances us from purpose:** Energy spent nurturing

bitterness is energy taken from growth. Job could not have stepped into restoration while clinging to resentment.

Job had every reason to feel justified in his pain. But justification doesn't lighten the load. It often adds to it. The weight grows until it starts defining us, making us smaller, angrier, harder.

Forgiveness isn't saying what happened didn't matter. It's telling you to refuse to carry the pain longer than you need to. When Job eventually prayed for his friends, it wasn't weakness. It was a strength. It was he setting down the weight he was never meant to carry.

The Decision to Forgive

Forgiveness doesn't always arrive with clarity. It doesn't always feel graceful. It often begins as a quiet nudge, an internal whisper suggesting it's time to let go of what's hurting you, even when nothing has been done right.

Job's friends had hurt him deeply. They questioned his integrity, misrepresented his pain, and compounded his suffering with their assumptions. After all that, they didn't apologize or take back their words. Yet Job did something radical: He chose to pray for them.
This wasn't a casual gesture. It was a pivotal moment, a

sacred turn in Job's story.

In that moment, forgiveness wasn't about how Job felt but about who he refused to become. It was a decision not to let their failure dictate his future, to release judgment, not because they earned it but because Job was ready to reclaim his peace.

At its core, forgiveness is a courageous act that defies logic and tells a better story.

Job could have waited for justice. He could have demanded restitution. He could have clung to bitterness and been justified in doing so, but instead, he forgave through prayer. Not performatively. Not out of obligation, but from a deep and private place where mercy lives.

Forbearing one another, and forgiving
one another, if any man have a quarrel against any:
even as Christ forgave you, so also do ye.
Colossians 3:13

When we choose to forgive, especially when nothing has been resolved, we take back our power. We make space for healing. We open the door to restoration, not just of relationships, but of ourselves.

Forgiveness doesn't mean the pain didn't matter. It means it no longer controls your next step, and for Job, that step became the beginning of restoration.

Forgiveness and Restoration

Forgiveness wasn't the end of Job's story. It was the key that unlocked a new beginning. It was the final act in a long, painful chapter of loss, silence, misunderstanding, and the first step into a future marked by renewal, blessing, and peace.

For so long, Job had endured, physically broken, emotionally isolated, and spiritually exhausted. He had wrestled with God and with himself. He had lost nearly everything. It wasn't until he prayed for his friends, those who had hurt him, that the narrative shifted.

That moment was not just a line in the story but a turning point. The act of forgiving was a spiritual breakthrough. It released something not only over his relationships but over his entire life.

When Job chose to pray for those who misjudged and disappointed him, something profound happened: his healing deepened. His restoration began. Not because his friends deserved it, everything made sense, but because Job's heart could bless those who once wounded him.

Why Forgiveness Precedes Restoration

Forgiveness clears space. Where bitterness resides, blessing cannot dwell. Where grudges grow, growth is stunted. The heart cannot carry both resentment and renewal. One always suffocates the other.

Restoration isn't just about what comes back to you; it's about who you've become by the time it arrives. And if the pain has shaped you, but bitterness still chains you, you'll miss the full beauty of what was always meant to be yours.

Job didn't manipulate this moment. He didn't forgive to get something. He forgave because mercy had found its home in him, and the result. Everything changed.

- His body was renewed.
- His fortune was restored.
- His relationships were reestablished.
- His influence returned with greater depth.

None of that came before forgiveness. Forgiveness wasn't a side note—it was the gate.

Are You Standing in the Way of Your Restoration?
Sometimes, what keeps us stuck is not what was done to us, it's what we're still holding on to; the offense, the anger, the quiet vow never to forget or release. That pain

becomes part of our identity, and we cling to it, afraid that letting it go means letting them win.

Here's the truth: you don't forgive to set them free. You forgive to set yourself free.

You may be praying for restoration, hoping for change, or believing for a breakthrough. However, if bitterness still occupies the places meant for healing, restoration will feel delayed because it is.

And be ye kind one to another,
tenderhearted, forgiving one another,
even as God for Christ's sake
hath forgiven you.
Ephesians 4:32

Restoration begins when you say, "This pain no longer defines me." It starts when you open your hands and release the weight of who hurt you, what they said, how they judged, or what they failed to be.

Job's story invites you to examine your own heart:

- Who have you not forgiven?
- What resentment still lingers in the background of your healing?
- Where do you need to release so that restoration can begin?

You don't have to feel ready. You just have to choose it. Forgiveness may not come all at once, but the moment you begin, the doors of renewal start to open.

What Forgiveness Is, and Isn't

Forgiveness is one of the most potent acts a person can offer, but it is also one of the most misunderstood. Many people resist forgiveness because they confuse it with things it is not. Forgiveness can be misrepresented as weakness, denial, or a free pass. But at its core, forgiveness is strength, clarity, and healing.

To walk in freedom, we must understand what forgiveness truly means, and just as importantly, what it does not mean.

Forgiveness IS NOT:

- **Forgetting:** Forgiveness doesn't erase the memory of what happened. It doesn't wipe clean the timeline or pretend the pain never existed. Forgetting is often impossible, and it's not the goal. The memory may remain, but the grip of that memory begins to loosen.
- **Excusing:** Forgiveness does not say, "What you did was okay." It does not downplay harm or dismiss injustice. It simply means you are no longer allowing that harm to hold your life hostage.
- **Reconciliation without boundaries:** Forgiveness and reconciliation are not the same. You can forgive some-

one without inviting them back into your life. Reconciliation requires mutual work and safety; forgiveness requires only your willingness to release.

- **Ignoring your pain:** Forgiveness doesn't mean silencing your hurt. It often requires confronting it. You cannot forgive what you haven't acknowledged.
- **A one-time emotional shift:** Forgiveness is not always a single, sweeping act. Sometimes, it's daily, and sometimes, it's layered. It may begin as a decision and be followed by a process.

Forgiveness IS:

- **Releasing control:** It's letting go of your right to make the offender suffer. It's surrendering the burden of trying to balance the scales. You stop replaying the offense and start reclaiming your energy.
- **Creating space for your healing:** When you forgive, you clear out the toxic residue of betrayal or harm. It's not about the offender; it's about your wholeness.
- **Choosing peace over resentment:** Bitterness may feel justified, but it drains life from the soul. Forgiveness chooses to pursue peace instead of keeping score.
- **Breaking the power of the past:** If you are tethered to what someone did to you, you're living in reaction to them. Forgiveness severs that tether. It gives you back your direction.
- **Strengthening your emotional integrity:** When you forgive, you are not denying the pain. You are affirming your worth. You are saying I deserve a life that isn't defined by what was done to me.

Forgiveness is not a denial of justice, but a declaration that your healing matters more than your hurt. It is not an endorsement of pain, but a protest against its control. Forgiveness makes room for joy, peace, clarity, and forward motion; in Job's case, it made room for restoration.

The Ripple Effect of Forgiveness

Forgiveness is never just a personal act; it's a generational one. What begins as an internal decision can influence everyone around us. It reshapes atmospheres, repairs broken lines, and redefines what flows from our lives.

Job's decision to forgive his friends impacted him and his future. His life began to turn when he chose to pray for those who misjudged him. Restoration followed not only in material things but also in relationships, clarity, and peace. Forgiveness set in motion a ripple of redemption.

What if your decision to forgive could be the turning point for you, your family, your marriage, and your community?

What Forgiveness Sets in Motion

- **Healing for Yourself:** The first ripple is internal. The emotional burden lightens. Peace re-enters the heart. The mind is freed to dream again.
- **Influence over Atmosphere:** Forgiveness changes how we speak, lead, and love. It softens our tone and in-

creases our compassion. Our energy shifts, and others notice.

- **Permission for Others to Heal:** When people witness forgiveness, it inspires them to release their grudges. Your example becomes a mirror in which others see possibility.
- **Reconnection in Relationships:** Not every relationship will be restored, but some may. Forgiveness creates the only climate in which reconciliation can even become possible.
- **Spiritual Clarity:** Bitterness fogs perspective. Forgiveness opens the way for insight, faith, and alignment with deeper truth.
- **Legacy:** Children watch how we handle pain. Friends absorb how we move through conflict. Communities are shaped by the stories we tell. When forgiveness is part of our story, it becomes part of what we pass on.

Forgiveness is like a stone cast into still waters. The ripples move outward, beyond what we can see.

Sometimes, just like Job, that simple act of release becomes the catalyst for everything we've been waiting for.

Moving Forward Without Bitterness

The hardest part of forgiveness isn't always the moment you decide to let go—it's the commitment to keep living free. Bitterness can return in quiet moments when memories rise, when wounds feel fresh. When something reminds you of how deeply you were wronged.

Job could have forgiven his friends once, but then fallen back into resentment every time he remembered their words, but he chose to move forward without bitterness. He didn't carry what had been said or done into his new season. He didn't let old accusations taint new beginnings.

To move forward without bitterness means refusing to rehearse the pain. It means reminding yourself that while you may still remember, you are no longer bound. It's a decision to choose peace over proof, healing over hostility.

Bitterness looks for validation. Freedom looks for peace.

Bitterness expects compensation. Freedom trusts restoration.

Bitterness chains you to the past. Freedom opens you to the future.

You may not be able to control how others respond,

apologize, or change, but you can choose what you carry, and the lighter your soul, the farther you can go.

Bitterness is a thief of destiny. Forgiveness reclaims it. Let the past inform you but not imprison you. Let it teach you but not tether you.

Restorative forgiveness is not about pretending the pain never happened. It's about refusing to let it write the final chapter. When Job forgave, he didn't rewrite history. He rewrote the future. His act of mercy opened a floodgate of healing, not just for him but for all connected to him.

You have the same power to stop the cycle, release the weight, and walk into restoration without dragging bitterness behind you. This is your turning point. not because they earned it, but because you are ready to be whole.

"The end of the matter is often better than its beginning—not because it's easier, but because it's refined

chapter eight
Restored Beyond Measure

Beyond What Was Lost

When we think of restoration, we often imagine returning what was taken from us. We long for familiar shapes to return, relationships to heal the same way, opportunities to return just as they were, and losses to be repaid in the currency they were taken. However, Job's story shows us that real restoration doesn't work that way.

Job's restoration wasn't just about reclaiming wealth or comfort. It was about becoming someone he could not have been without the pain. He didn't just receive double for his trouble; he received more profound clarity, peace, and expansive influence.

After the storm, Job's wealth increased, but more importantly, his insight deepened. His once fractured friendships were refined. His perspective on life, God, and himself became rooted in something far more lasting than comfort. It was anchored in wisdom.

He had known prosperity before, but now he understood peace. He had known the community before, but now he had compassion. He had lived with influence before, but now he lived with humility.

This is the surprising nature of restoration: it comes in unfamiliar forms. We may ask for what we lost, only to be given what we didn't know we needed. It doesn't always arrive wrapped in the same packages. Sometimes, what we gain looks nothing like what we prayed for, but it's better.

- A renewed heart to see life through softer eyes.
- A rekindled sense of gratitude for moments once taken for granted.
- A capacity to lead not just from strength, but from empathy.
- A clearer vision of purpose, no longer shadowed by entitlement.

Restoration doesn't mean going backward. It means moving forward with new depth. Job's story wasn't about retrieving what once was. It was about receiving what never could have come without the storm.

That's what makes the end of the matter better than its beginning, not because it's easier, but because it's refined.

A Heart Changed Before a Life Rebuilt

The most powerful restorations begin inside. Something within him had already transformed before anything in Job's world shifted. His journey through loss, abandonment, and silence had carved out a new interior space filled with humility, perspective, and grace. He emerged not just waiting for restoration, but ready for it.

Before his fortune returned, Job had already released bitterness. Before his body was renewed, his heart had softened. Before his relationships were mended, he had chosen forgiveness. These were not small shifts; they were the groundwork for lasting change.

Too often, we expect life to fix the outside so we can feel whole on the inside, but Job's story reveals the reverse. The inward alignment, surrender, healing, and perspective pave the way for the visible restoration.

This kind of heart work is deep. It requires honesty, reflection, and the courage to let go of narratives that no longer serve us, but it also produces the kind of character that can carry abundance without arrogance and blessing without entitlement.

Had Job received everything without being changed, he might have simply returned to life as usual, but because his heart had been refined through pain, what he received didn't just restore him. It repositioned him.

He was no longer a man merely blessed by circumstance. He was a man marked by grace. This is why the internal work matters so deeply, because restoration that outpaces character eventually becomes a burden, but when the heart is ready, the rebuilding becomes sacred.

So, if it feels like the rebuilding hasn't started yet, take courage. Maybe something greater is being constructed inside you, and when the time is right, it won't just be life that is restored; it will be you.

The Redemption of Time

Time is one of the most painful casualties of loss. When we suffer, it often feels like the months or even years spent in pain were stolen from us. We look back and wonder what could have been if the crisis hadn't occurred. We grieve not just what happened, but all the opportunities passed us by while trying to survive.

Job's story speaks directly to this sorrow. His suffering was not momentary; it stretched across time. The days were long, and the nights even longer. His body was failing, his friends were silent or condemning, and heaven felt withdrawn. Living through such a season often leaves a

person convinced that time has been wasted.
Then something extraordinary happened.

After Job forgave his friends and let go of bitterness, restoration began, not just in the physical realm but also in the realm of time. He was granted a long life, peace, and the joy of watching multiple generations come after him. The years that seemed lost were redeemed, not by erasing the past but by filling the future with meaning.

This is what the redemption of time looks like. It's not always about getting back what was taken; it's about receiving something richer in the seasons ahead. It's about a peace that softens what once felt like stolen time. It's the joy of realizing the story wasn't over, even when it felt like it had ended.

Time redeemed doesn't always mean time replaced. It implies time repurposed.

- The lessons learned in the valley shape wisdom for the mountaintop.
- The compassion born through suffering becomes a lifeline for others.
- The stillness, once filled with sorrow, becomes a sacred reflection.

For Job, seeing his children, grandchildren, and great-grandchildren wasn't just a biological blessing but an emotional restoration. Witnessing a legacy rise from the ashes was like waking up each morning knowing that the purpose continued.

To anyone who feels that too much time has passed, that too much was lost, remember this: You're not too late. Your best days are not behind you. What felt like a pause might have been preparation, and what seemed like a detour could become the most powerful stretch of your journey.

In the hands of grace, time is never wasted. It is reclaimed, reimagined, and rewritten.

Wholeness over Replacement

When we experience profound loss, it's natural to want everything restored exactly as it was. We long for our relationships, the routines we once knew, and the sense of stability that once anchored us. However, Job's story teaches us something far more powerful: the goal of restoration is not replacement, it is wholeness.

Job received double what he had lost: livestock, wealth, and standing in the community, but it wasn't the same livestock, the same comforts, or the same children. What was returned to him didn't erase what he had grieved, but became part of something whole, complete, and meaningful.

This restoration honours both what was lost and what can still be gained. It doesn't pretend that pain didn't happen. Instead, it weaves the pain into a new story where the scars are part of the beauty.

What Wholeness Looks Like

- **Emotional Peace:** Wholeness doesn't mean you forget the pain. It means you're no longer fighting it every day. It means you've made peace with your journey and no longer carry the weight of trying to change the past.
- **Reordered Priorities:** After the loss, what mattered most to Job shifted. True wholeness clarifies what truly counts: faith, love, people, and integrity. It strips away the superficial and strengthens what's eternal.
- **Resilience without Bitterness:** Job's story didn't make him harder; it made him wiser. Wholeness means you can carry strength without closing your heart. It means you emerge with grace, not just grit.
- **Deeper Compassion:** The pain Job endured likely made him more empathetic toward others. Wholeness transforms suffering into softness toward others' suffering. It deepens our ability to care.
- **Purpose that Transcends Possessions:** While Job regained material wealth, the actual restoration was internal. Wholeness means your purpose no longer depends on external success. It lives in who you've become.

When you aim for replacement, you stay attached to what

was. When you pursue wholeness, you become available to what can be.

Wholeness says, "I may never get back exactly what I lost, but I can move forward as someone more whole, wiser, and more at peace." Let that be your aim.

The Blessing of a Softened Heart

Perhaps the most overlooked part of Job's restoration was not in his fortune or family but in his spirit. The man who had every reason to grow cold and guarded emerged from his suffering tender and whole. That, more than anything, was his most significant gain.

When pain strikes, there's a temptation to harden. We shield ourselves from future harm. We put walls around our hearts, convinced they'll protect us, but in truth, those walls often keep healing out, they barricade joy, trust, and connection.

Job didn't let that happen. Instead of turning inward and bitter, he chose mercy. Instead of shrinking from others, he prayed for those who misunderstood him. His wealth returned, but it came to a man who had not allowed bitterness to rob him of gentleness.

This is the true blessing of a softened heart: to feel again without fear, to lead without pride, and to love without condition.

Signs of a Softened Heart:

- You respond gracefully rather than retaliate, even when others don't deserve it.
- You listen deeply instead of jumping to defend because you've known the ache of being unheard.
- You weep more easily, love more fiercely, and give more freely because you understand what lacking means.
- You hold space for others in their suffering because you haven't forgotten your own.
- You embrace simplicity with joy because you've seen how fleeting the superficial can be.

This soft, open-heart posture is evidence that pain did not win. It's the proof that the journey refined rather than ruined you. For Job, restoration wasn't just about what he received. It was about who he became, and that is the highest restoration of all.

Your Turn: Restoration as a Personal Promise

Job's story was not preserved in history merely to inspire; it was written to awaken hope. His path from devastation to restoration is a miracle of the past and a living example of what's still possible.

You may not know how or when restoration will come, but this is true: healing is never off the table. Renewal is still on the horizon, and wholeness, though it may come in a different form than you imagined, is within reach.

What Job gained wasn't just material. He gained clarity, compassion, and connection to something deeper than comfort: purpose. His restoration reminds us that we don't have to be defined by what we lost, but by how we rise from it.

If you've endured heartbreak, silence, the sting of misjudgement, or the ache of loss, know you're still here, and that means restoration is still possible.

Start by believing that your story is not over.

Begin by surrendering the belief that you are too broken to be made whole again.

Restoration may not replicate the past, but it will redeem it. It may not undo the pain, but it can use it.

Think of the mother who, after years of infertility and heartbreak, finds herself mentoring and supporting other women walking the same painful path. Restoration.

Think of the entrepreneur who lost everything in a financial crash, only to return with a business grounded in purpose and empathy. Restoration.

Think of the man who grew up fatherless but became the nurturing presence his children and others never had. Restoration.

Think of the woman who survived betrayal, not by pretending it didn't hurt, but by using her story to help others heal. Restoration.

These stories aren't perfect. They don't erase pain, but they point to what Job's life proclaimed: what has been torn can be rewoven. What has been emptied can be filled, and what has been crushed can rise again, firmer, softer, and more beautiful.
This is your turning point. This is your moment to believe again. This is your chapter of gain, even after great pain.

Conclusion
A Legacy of Grace

The journey through pain is never easy. It tests every fibre of our being, every corner of our faith, and every ounce of our strength, but as we've seen through Job's life and throughout this series, pain is not the period at the end of our story. It is often the comma before the greatest turning point.

Job didn't just survive his season of suffering. He emerged restored, refined, and realigned. His life, once known for its abundance, became known for something even greater: its transformation.

This is where legacy begins.

Legacy is not what we accumulate. It's what we awaken in others. It's the resilience we model. The grace we extend, the hope we refuse to surrender.

In Job's story, we see the blueprint of a life that moved from brokenness to blessing, not because the pain vanished, but because he refused to be reduced by it. He rose from the ashes of despair with a heart more open, a spirit more grounded, and a testimony more potent than his prosperity ever was.

You've now walked through three lives in this series: Joseph, Jesus, and Job, each marked by intense pain, betrayal, isolation, or loss. Yet in every story, the pain was not wasted. It was woven. It worked. It was used to bring about a gain that far outweighed the loss.

Joseph turned betrayal into destiny.
Jesus turned suffering into salvation.
Job turned sorrow into a legacy.

So what about you?

What if your pain isn't just something to endure, but something that holds the seed of purpose? What if everything you've walked through prepares you for something far greater than you can imagine?

Let this be your takeaway: You don't have to escape your pain to gain something from it. You only need to surrender it. Let it shape you. Let it teach you. Let it transform you, because the story doesn't end in ashes when pain is met with purpose.

It ends in glory.

Your legacy will be in what you built and in how you rose, loved, forgave, and lived fully again.

This is the legacy of grace, and it can be yours, too.

The Author

Biodun Olaitan is an insightful teacher, Preacher and qualified life and marriage Coach. He is the Lead Pastor of RCCG CRA COVENTRY in the United Kingdom.

A trained Church management consultant and graduate of Leadership and Management from the Staffordshire University. He is an author of several books including: *"5 Essentials keys to Success" and "There shall be a performance".*

He is married to Adejoke, who Pastors with him, and their union is blessed with two beautiful daughters and grandchildren.

OTHER PRODUCTS

BY BIODUN OLAITAN

Scan this QRCode for more